JIMMY CARTER, PRESIDENT

Betsy Covington Smith

Walker and Company
New York

*In memory of
another Southerner, my father,
William Slaughter Covington
1897–1985*

First published in the United States of America
in 1986 by the Walker Publishing Company, Inc.

Published simultaneously in Canada by John Wiley & Sons
Canada, Limited, Rexdale, Ontario.

Library of Congress Cataloging-in-Publication Data

Smith, Betsy Covington.
  Jimmy Carter, President.

  (Presidential biography series)
  Includes index.
  Summary: Follows the life and career of the peanut
farmer who became Governor of Georgia and then the
thirty-ninth President.
  1. Carter, Jimmy, 1924–   —Juvenile literature.
2. Presidents—United States—Biography—Juvenile
literature. [1. Carter, Jimmy, 1924–
2. Presidents] I. Title.   II. Series.
E873.S64   1986   973.926′092′4   [B]   [92]   86-5589
ISBN 0-8027-6650-1
ISBN 0-8027-6652-8 (lib. bdg.)

Book Design by Teresa M. Carboni

Printed in the United States of America

10 9 8 7 6 5 4 3 2

Contents

Acknowledgments

The author gratefully acknowledges the use of the following sources in researching this book: *Keeping Faith: Memoirs of a President* by Jimmy Carter; *First Lady from Plains* by Rosalynn Carter; *Dasher—The Roots and Rising of Jimmy Carter* by James Wooten; "The Enigmatic President" by Hedley Donovan, as reprinted in *Time* magazine, 6 May 1985, from the author's book *Roosevelt to Reagan: A Reporter's Encounters with Nine Presidents*. The author also wishes to thank Messrs. Robert Bohanan and David Alsobrook of the Carter Presidential Materials Staff for their assistance in supplying presidential photographs for this book.

1

One Day in April

April 24, 1980, seemed a rather routine day in the White House. President Carter was hard at work. He met with congressional leaders to discuss legislation; he spoke privately with Israeli Labor party leader, Shimon Peres; he briefed a group of Hispanic leaders on his anti-inflation program. To the hundreds of journalists in Washington that day, men and women trained to sniff out news before it broke, there were no signs that anything out of the ordinary might happen.

That was exactly how the president had wanted the day to appear. Yet as he and only a few of his closest advisers knew, that day would be anything but humdrum. On that April morning in Washington, night had already fallen in the Middle East, and under the cover of darkness eight American helicopters were secretly on their way toward a remote area inside Iran. Their mission? To rescue the American hostages being held captive in Iran's capital city of Tehran.

More than five months had passed since the president had learned that the U.S. Embassy had been overrun by three thousand angry Iranian militants who had captured "fifty or sixty" Americans. These militants, largely students, hated the United States. They vowed to hold the hostages until their despised former ruler, the shah of

1

President Carter at work in the Oval Office.

Iran, was forced to return home to stand trial. They also demanded that the vast amount of money that the shah and his family were said to have taken with them when they fled Iran be returned. If these conditions were not met, they screamed to a stunned world, the hostages would be forced to stand trial for crimes against Iran. If guilty, they would be put to death.

Americans held hostage? U.S. diplomats blindfolded and paraded before angry street mobs in downtown Tehran? The pictures that flashed across American television screens those first few weeks were horrifying and humiliating. But at first almost everybody, including President Carter, had thought that the crisis would not last long. After all, there had never been a government anywhere in the world that had failed to protect foreign diplomats.

A blindfolded American hostage is paraded before the crowds in Tehran.

But that was the problem. Who *was* in charge in Iran? Where were the normal diplomatic channels? Ever since the shah, a good friend of the United States, had been forced to flee eight months earlier, there had been neither a stable government nor any strong government leaders. Instead, the most powerful figure to emerge after the shah was an aged, fanatical religious leader, the Ayatollah Khomeini. Having spent fifteen years in exile, Khomeini had returned to his country shortly after the shah had departed. To the millions of Iranians who had wept and cheered at his arrival, he had become a martyr. His intense hatred of both the shah and the United States soon became a frenzied echo that reverberated throughout the streets of Tehran. This hatred had finally erupted with the seizure of the U.S. Embassy.

3

The Ayatollah Khomeini blesses his followers in Iran.

And so America's ordeal had begun. For President Carter, the man who bore responsibility for bringing the hostages safely home, the situation was especially anguishing. "The first week of November 1979 marked the beginning of the most difficult period of my life," he wrote later in his memoirs. "The safety and well-being of the American hostages became a constant concern for me, no matter what other duties I was performing as president."

Short of all-out military intervention, which would have killed the hostages and thousands of other innocent people,

President Carter pursued every conceivable tactic to end the crisis. He expelled all Iranian students, many of whom hadn't been in school in years, who were in the United States illegally. He banned the purchase of Iranian oil. He made plans to seize all Iranian assets in the United States, which totaled $12 billion. He threatened to close Iranian seaports. He asked the pope to intervene with the Ayatollah Khomeini, and he persuaded Secretary General of the United Nations Kurt Waldheim to go to Iran to negotiate for the hostages' release. In addition, secret agents were sent into Iran; satellite photographs were taken of the U.S.

Iranian demonstrators burn the American flag to show their hatred of the United States.

Embassy as well as of Iranian military installations; and intermediaries from other countries were used to negotiate secretly with Iranian officials.

Nothing worked. As the days passed into weeks and then stretched into months, the president's hopes rose and fell. Just as it looked as if one or another scheme for ending the crisis would be successful, something would happen to sabotage the plan, leaving the captured Americans no closer to freedom than before. By April the situation looked as dismal as ever. Then, unexpectedly, there was a new threat. Neighboring Iraq began to look as if it might invade Iran. The short entry in Jimmy Carter's personal diary at that time clearly bore the words of a discouraged man:

> The Iranians are making all kinds of crazy threats to kill the American hostages if they are invaded by Iraq — whom they identify as an American puppet.
>
> April 10, 1980

It was time to act. Then. After so many failed diplomatic attempts, the president decided the time had come to go in and bring the hostages home.

Plans for a rescue operation actually had begun only two days after the U.S. Embassy had been seized. At that time, however, a successful rescue attempt appeared impossible because the embassy was in a heavily populated area of downtown Tehran and the nearest U.S. aircraft carriers were more than six hundred miles away. How could a rescue team be flown into Tehran unnoticed and penetrate the embassy? And could the large group of hostages and rescuers manage to slip out of the country without anyone knowing?

By April the answers were clearer. Now the United States had detailed blueprints of all the embassy buildings in Tehran. The CIA also had secret information about the locations of every hostage, the number and placement of every guard, and the twenty-four-hour schedule of both

President Carter meets with the worried wives and families of the Americans being held hostage in Iran in 1980.

hostages and guards. What's more, America's military leaders had seen to it that extensive training and preparation for a rescue mission had been done.

Meeting with the president, the mission commanders of the rescue operation, Generals James Vaught and Philip Gast and Col. Charles Beckwith, presented the rescue plan: seven (later eight) helicopters would fly from U.S. aircraft carriers in the Gulf of Oman to a remote area in Iran, already checked out in an earlier secret mission. There the helicopters would be joined by six C-130 transport planes carrying a ninety-member rescue team as well as fuel and supplies. The men in the airplanes would then board the helicopters. While the transport planes quickly flew out of Iran, the helicopters, then carrying the rescue team, would fly on to a specified place in some nearby mountains. There the men and the helicopters would hide during the approaching daylight hours.

The next night, trucks that had been bought earlier by U.S. secret agents would be removed from a warehouse on the outskirts of Tehran. They would then be driven to a designated spot near the rescue team's hiding place where they'd pick up the rescuers and take them to the city. Then the actual rescue would begin. Simultaneously, members of the team would enter both the foreign ministry building, where three hostages were being held, and the embassy compound. They would quickly overpower the guards and free the captives. With precision timing, the helicopters would land in the compound and both rescuers and hostages would scramble aboard and be flown to an abandoned airstrip near the city where two C-141s would be waiting to take them across the Iranian border to safety.

The plan had all the elements of an exciting TV action film: good guys and bad guys, an exotic foreign location, secret agents, whirling helicopters, a daring escape under the cover of night. But this was no Hollywood thriller. It was real. Its plot had been worked out in detail by the best minds in the U.S. military. Its actors were brave, highly trained men who would be in a life-and-death situation. Its outcome would be judged by an audience made up of the entire world population. If it was a success, it would erase the humiliation that Americans had suffered during the months the hostages had been held captive. If it failed, people everywhere would see the United States as a pathetic, clumsy giant. Even worse, the lives of the hostages would be in the gravest possible danger.

No one knew better than Jimmy Carter how much was at stake. Yet after questioning the military leaders about every facet of the plan, he felt satisfied. He gave them his complete approval. "Because I was so clear in my resolve," he said later, "I looked forward to the mission."

On the morning of April 24, President Carter tried to appear as relaxed as possible. It was hard. But as president, he knew he was in the spotlight. Any break in his normal routine or slip of the tongue could instantly alert the Iranians and endanger the lives of the hostages.

By midmorning the first bit of news from the Middle East came in and was quietly relayed to the president by National Security Adviser Zbigniew Brzezinski. So far so good. The eight helicopters had taken off as planned and were on their way to Desert One, the designated landing spot in Iran.

At noon Carter had lunch with Vice President Mondale, Secretary of State Cyrus Vance, Secretary of Defense Harold Brown, his two closest aides, Hamilton Jordan and Jody Powell, and Brzezinski, all of whom had been in on the rescue plans. Although it was still too early to know for certain, the news was worrisome. The helicopters had run into severe local dust storms. Two of them were down. The remaining six—the minimum needed for the mission— were apparently proceeding onward.

By midafternoon reports came in more frequently. The C-130 transport planes and the six helicopters had landed. Almost immediately, however, they had met a totally unexpected problem. On a remote road near the landing site, which U.S. agents had previously described as being free of any traffic, three Iranian motor vehicles had suddenly appeared. The first was a bus filled with forty passengers. It had been stopped and its passengers detained. Then came a fuel truck and a pickup truck, which had taken off across the desert and escaped. Would the drivers of these trucks report the Americans' presence? It was a possibility. To prevent the detained bus passengers from sounding an alarm, President Carter approved the idea of flying them all to Egypt until the rescue was completed.

An hour later the news was good. All six helicopters had been refueled and were ready to take the rescue team to their hiding place in the mountains.

But twenty minutes later, word came that one of the helicopters had developed hydraulic problems, leaving operable only five helicopters, one less than the minimum number needed. Should they risk going ahead anyway? Colonel Beckwith, on the ground in Iran, and General

Vaught, monitoring the mission from Egypt, recommended that the remainder of the mission be scrapped. At 4:57 P.M. in Washington, just as daylight was about to break in Iran, President Carter turned to Secretary of Defense Brown and said decisively, "Let's go with his recommendation." With that, the entire mission came to an end.

All the planning, all the suspense, all the hopes of rescuing the hostages had been dashed. It was a terrible disappointment. Still, it wasn't the worst thing that could have happened. The rescue crew would then depart aboard the transport planes and, later, the Iranians would certainly make a hullabaloo about the abandoned U.S. helicopters. But Iranian anger wouldn't be anything new. The important thing was that no lives had been lost in the mission. That's all that really mattered to the president.

Suddenly, like a horror film unraveling without a plot, new reports began coming in. There had been a collision at the landing site! In moving away from the loaded transport planes for takeoff, the helicopters had kicked up great clouds of dust, which had made visibility on the ground very poor. Incredibly, one of the helicopters had then plowed into the nose of one of the C-130s. Both aircraft had burst into flames. It wasn't until hours later, nearly midnight in Washington, that the full extent of the tragedy was confirmed—eight Americans dead and three badly burned. Everyone else had been flown safely out of the country.

Through an almost incredible series of unforeseen mishaps, a day that had begun with such high hopes had ended in shambles. Not only had eight brave men lost their lives on a lonely Iranian desert, but the mighty United States was sure to look ridiculous. After only a couple of hours' sleep, an anguished President Carter gave a brief public statement the following morning. He outlined what had happened, gave his reasons for attempting the mission, and took full responsibility for its failure.

For those who had followed Jimmy Carter's amazing rise from nowhere to the presidency of the most powerful nation in the world, there was something cruelly ironic about the failed rescue mission. Throughout the fifty-five years of his life, Jimmy Carter had seldom failed at anything. As a former naval officer and engineer, he had always believed that hard work and systematic planning, including close attention to detail, could solve any problem. These were the things that had accounted for his successes. But here he was now, the man responsible for a mission beset by so many awful surprises and bungled details that it looked as if it had been conceived and carried out by children.

The failed rescue attempt of the American hostages in Iran was the beginning of the end of the presidency of Jimmy Carter, the thirty-ninth president of the United States. Six months later, when Americans flocked to the polls, it became clear that not enough time had elapsed for them to forget or forgive what had happened on that humiliating day earlier in the year.

Thus, Jimmy Carter from Plains, Georgia, one of the most intelligent, fascinating, and baffling presidents in American history, was retired from office after a single term.

2

The Boy from Plains

Jimmy Who? they called him, and for good reason. When Jimmy Carter joined the pack of Democratic contenders for the 1976 presidential nomination, millions of Americans had never heard of him. Even today, years after he's been out of office, he remains Jimmy Who? in many people's minds — one of the most unique and puzzling figures in American presidential history.

Any understanding of Jimmy Carter must begin in the tiny, southwest Georgia town of Plains. For it was there that he was born, grew up, and spent nine years of his adult life. That alone makes him unique. For although other U.S. presidents have come from small towns, no one else had spent so many adult years in such a setting. Carter's roots in Georgia were strong and deep. His family had originated in Virginia with the arrival in 1637 of Thomas Carter, a colonist from England. Like other early colonists, the Carter family then spread out, some settling in eastern North Carolina, others going farther south. Two hundred years ago, Jimmy Carter's ancestor Kindred Carter arrived in Georgia. There he stayed, having found

Jimmy Carter, six months old, with his mother.

what he'd been looking for—good, rich soil and lush forests that could be easily cleared, planted, and tilled. When Kindred Carter died in 1800, he left to his family three hundred acres suitable for growing cotton and wheat and for raising horses, cattle, mules, and pigs.

Farming was the work of the Carter family for generations. As the Carter sons grew to manhood, they branched into other Georgia counties where they bought more land and raised families of their own. Although the Civil War temporarily interrupted their prosperity, in time they rebuilt their holdings. The Carters, after all, were known to be hard workers.

The first of the Carter family to move to tiny Plains was James Earl, who came there as a boy in 1904 with his widowed mother and his brother, Alton. After military duty in World War I, Earl returned to Plains where he met, fell in love with, and in 1923 married Lillian Gordy, a pretty, vivacious nursing student at the Plains Hospital. On October 1, 1924, their first child, James Earl Carter, Jr., was born. His delighted parents immediately began calling him Jimmy.

The future president began life in a rented house in Plains. When he was four, he and his parents and his little sister, Gloria, born when he was two, moved to a larger house on a farm that his father had bought before his marriage. Just outside Plains, the farm bordered a black community called Archery. After the family moved into the new house, Earl Carter opened a store on his land, stocking it with such rural staples as kerosene and lamp wicks, rattraps, tobacco, snuff, castor oil, seed, animal feed, soap, flour, overalls, and work boots.

Life for Lillian and Earl Carter and their two children was worlds apart from the way most families live today. Like most Southerners then, especially those in rural areas, they had no electricity and no plumbing and had to use a privy in the backyard. Their clapboard house was shaded by pecan, magnolia, fig, mulberry, and chinaberry trees, making it delightfully cool in the summer. But in winter, heat came only from two fireplaces and the kitchen stove. Often on frigid winter nights, Jimmy would fall asleep snuggled against warm bricks that had been heated on the stove, wrapped, and carried to his bed. Beyond the winter's discomfort, there were always chores that needed doing. Wood for the stove and fireplaces had to be chopped and sawed; kerosene lamps had to be filled nightly; and the yard around the house, consisting of sand rather than grass, had to be constantly swept.

"We weren't rich, but we weren't poor," Jimmy's mother, Lillian, has said. "We lived very, very well in terms of having what we wanted." Indeed, she and Earl had two possessions that were the envy of all Plains—a battery-operated radio and a Model A Ford that Earl had bought for three hundred and fifty dollars.

The person who had the earliest and strongest influence on Jimmy was his mother. Lillian Carter was a remarkable woman. In addition to having a fine mind and a good sense of humor, she had an insatiable curiosity to learn all she could about the world that stretched beyond Plains. An avid reader, she wanted her children to love books too, to know about and feel things that were beyond their immediate vision. (She had taught Jimmy to read by the time he was four.) Lillian, a deeply compassionate person, really cared about other human beings. At a time when white people and black people in the South lived a master-servant relationship with their lives and communities completely separate and segregated, she stood out because she was forever worrying and checking up on the various health problems of members of the black community.

Jimmy also looked up to his father. Earl was a hard worker who treated his farmhands well and ran his entire place with authority. His farm was similar to other large, successful Southern farms at that time. He had several hundred acres of land on which more than two hundred blacks lived rent-free. The men were paid $1.00 a day, the women $.75, the children $.25. The days were long, beginning with the bell that clanged at dawn, awakening the Carters and their farmhands, and ending with the plodding return home of the mule-drawn wagons along rutted dirt lanes. The major crops on the farm were cotton, peanuts, corn, watermelons, and potatoes.

In 1929, the year his second sister, Ruth, was born, Jimmy became a pint-sized, five-year-old entrepreneur. Every morning he would get up at dawn. Barefoot and shirtless, he'd pull his little wagon out to the peanut fields, tug at the peanuts till they were out of the ground, shake the dirt off their vines, then pile them into his wagon. Back home, he'd pull the nuts from the vines, wash them, and soak them overnight. The next morning he'd build a fire in the backyard and boil his peanuts in a black pot over the fire. That done, he'd carefully measure out half a pound of peanuts to put in each of twenty bags. After breakfast he would gather up the bags and set out on foot for Plains. There, by selling each bag for five cents, he'd usually make a dollar a day.

Life on the Carter farm, however, was far more than unending work. While Earl and Lillian gave frequent parties, filling the house with music, laughter, and dancing, Jimmy led a life of mischief and adventure. Lean and slightly built, with hair the color of straw and a freckled, sunburned face, he stood out among his friends, most of whom were black children from nearby Archery. Although black and white children never attended the same schools in the South in those days, they often played together as small children. So, although Jimmy attended an all-white elementary school in Plains from age six on, at home he ran in a pack with his black friends. Together they built tree houses, fished, hunted, rode horses and mules, fixed fences, fed the chickens, milked the cows, and ground sugarcane. It was an isolated world, a world where children could explore and run free. All around them, as far as the eye could see, stretched miles and miles of farmland. The only night sounds, as people, weary from the day's work, sat on their front porches, were the chirping of crickets and night birds, the occasional barking of dogs, the distant moan of a train heading for faraway cities such as Atlanta or Savannah.

Like many Southern boys, Jimmy dreamed of the wonders beyond southwest Georgia. He was fascinated by his uncle, Tom Gordy, his mother's younger brother, who was in the U.S. Navy. Postcards from Uncle Tom were a big event. With their stamps from exotic ports all over the world, they spoke of a life of unimaginable adventure. Even by the age of six, Jimmy was already thinking that one day he too would be a sailor and visit those places. In

Jimmy, age six, poses with his sister, Gloria, age four.

Daddy (Earl Carter) standing in the door of his store, next door to the family house, with his children. Left to right: Gloria (6), Ruth (13), Jimmy (8).

Jimmy at age twelve, posing with his two younger sisters.

fourth grade he began checking out books from the public library on the world's oceans. And before entering high school in the autumn of 1938, he wrote a letter to the United States Naval Academy in Annapolis, Maryland, asking for information about entrance requirements.

By then the Carter family was complete—a family of six. Billy Carter had been born in 1937, thirteen years after his older brother. Jimmy's habit of saving his earnings

"Hot" Carter, at thirteen.

had brought him enough money to buy five enormous bales of cotton. Although his father's farm was thriving, it was still the Depression and the price of cotton was low. So Jimmy had stored his cotton, waiting for prices to rise. Four years later he sold it at a good price, earning enough money to buy five small houses in Plains, which brought him a rental income of $16.50 each month.

Lillian and Earl Carter were as proud as could be of their oldest child, amazed by his energy and ingenuity, delighted by his laughter and infectious grin. Earl called him Hot, short for Hot Shot. When Jimmy began talking about going to the U.S. Naval Academy after high school, Earl was especially pleased, having been an officer during World War I. Knowing that the recommendation of a state politician could help his son's chances for admission to Annapolis, he began contributing money and building a relationship with the U.S. representative from his district, Congressman Stephen Pace.

When Jimmy entered Plains High School, he was pleased he could tell Miss Julia Coleman, superintendent of the Plains educational system, that he had finished all of Tolstoy's *War and Peace* over the summer. Everyone wanted Miss Julia's approval. She was one of those rare teachers people feel fortunate to have even once in the entire course of their schooling. Although she was interested in all of her students, she was especially drawn to those who were bright and inquisitive and motivated to learn. Constantly she challenged Jimmy to stretch his mind, giving him long reading lists and expecting a lot of him. Years later Jimmy still credited her for having played an important role in shaping his life. "She saw something in me, I think ... a hunger to learn."

Meanwhile, throughout his four years in high school, Jimmy worried about getting into Annapolis. Knowing that he was at a disadvantage because Plains High School lacked a full science curriculum, he tried to teach himself. "I don't recall seeing Jimmy without a book or several books in his hands or somewhere close by all during his

Jimmy (standing, top left) holds the American flag with a group at Plains High School.

high school days," his cousin Hugh recalled. Jimmy also worried about some of the Naval Academy's physical requirements. The admissions information mentioned that malocclusion, or overbite, might prevent admission. Would the academy feel that he had buck teeth and disqualify him? Also, the academy didn't want anyone with flat feet. Jimmy didn't know whether or not his were, so just in case, he spent hours and hours rolling the soles of his feet on soft drink bottles.

Still, he didn't worry all the time. Nor was he a grind all the time. An average athlete, he wasn't tall enough to star in basketball, but he made a respectable record as a track runner. Most of all, though, he liked the recreational pastimes of his childhood. As with all white Southern children then, upon reaching high school he and his former black friends no longer did things together. So Jimmy now fished, hunted, hiked, and went camping with his white friends. He also joined his father on many predawn hunting excursions, which gave a new man-to-man kind of closeness to their relationship.

Although Jimmy had always gotten along well with girls, he never showed serious interest in anyone until his senior year. The girl was Eloise Ratliff, a very pretty, dark-haired farmer's daughter with huge eyes and a ravishing smile. She too was one of Miss Julia Coleman's favorites, quick, bright, and disciplined, someone with whom Jimmy had been competing since the start of high school. But at sixteen, when he graduated, he, not Eloise, emerged as top student in the class. By the narrowest of margins, he was named valedictorian of the class of 1941 while she was made salutatorian.

Yet Jimmy almost didn't graduate. During the final week of school, he and several other boys decided to play hooky. Hitchhiking to Americus, the nearest large town, they were caught, hauled back to Plains, and given a stern ultimatum. "We either had to take a licking or not graduate," Jimmy recalled years later with a smile. "The fellow who was going to give the punishment was very handy with the paddle and some of us gave serious consideration to becoming dropouts the week before graduation. But, in the end, we decided to take the punishment—and that's exactly where we took it: in the end."

Indeed, Jimmy's graduation was an end, an end to a wonderfully safe and insular childhood. But it was also a beginning, a start of a life even more challenging and exciting than the boy from Plains ever could have dreamed.

3
Moving On

To Jimmy's bitter disappointment, graduation did not lead directly to Annapolis. That following fall he went off to tiny Southwestern College, a poorly funded junior college in nearby Americus.

Initially he'd been awarded a scholarship to Southwestern for being the top student in his graduating class. Certain that he would be entering the academy, however, he'd given the scholarship to his friend, Eloise Ratliff, who desperately wanted to go to college but couldn't afford it. Then bad news had come from Congressman Pace; he had not been able to arrange Jimmy's appointment. He advised the sixteen year old to wait and try again after a year of college that would give him a better background in science. So, dejectedly, Jimmy went as a paying student to Southwestern.

The following year the news was good, but not nearly as good as Jimmy had hoped. Yes, wrote Congressman Pace, Jimmy's appointment to the U.S. Naval Academy had finally come through, but it wouldn't be for that year, 1942, but rather for the following summer in 1943. To Jimmy the delay seemed interminable. By then the United States had entered World War II and he longed to be among the elite corps of future naval officers training at Annapolis to fight in it. On the advice of one of his teachers at Southwestern, he finally decided to further prepare for Annapolis by transferring to the Georgia Institute of Technology in Atlanta, which had a naval ROTC program.

The year at Georgia Tech was far more rewarding than Jimmy had expected. The work was challenging and hard—much harder, he would later say, than that at Annapolis. Taking several math and engineering courses, which had been unavailable to him in either Miss Coleman's classes in Plains or at the tiny college in Americus, he impressed his classmates and teachers with his steadiness and his determination to succeed. Farther away from home than ever before, he moved easily into an active social life, which included rooting for the superb Georgia Tech football team, dating coeds, and going to college parties. In addition, he pursued a daily schedule of intramural sports and calisthenics as part of the ROTC program, the kind of physical exercise that would become even more rigorous, he knew, at Annapolis. Finally the news he had waited so long to hear arrived—the letter saying he was to report to Annapolis in June. It was, he said, "a dream come true."

When Jimmy arrived at Annapolis early that summer of 1943, he looked almost as if he were still a little boy. At nineteen, he stood five foot six and weighed less than 130 pounds. Like the almost one thousand other students entering Annapolis for the first time, the boy from Plains was overwhelmed by what he saw. On the three-hundred-acre campus sat Bancraft Hall, the world's largest dormitory and the center of life at the academy. It was here that all the students lived, scattered about in two thousand rooms located in four mammoth wings. It was here, too, that everyone gathered for meals three times a day in a mess hall that seated four thousand people.

At Annapolis, Jimmy immediately acquired the new name, "Plebe," the academy's designation for all first-year students. Because plebes were considered the lowest form of human life, they were subjected to a nonstop barrage of hazing, humiliation, and insults from upperclassmen. At mealtimes, for instance, plebes sometimes weren't allowed to eat at all, or they wouldn't be allowed to sit down, or they would be ordered to eat crouched beneath the table at the upperclassmen's feet. No plebe was allowed a moment's peace night or day for one solid year. Some couldn't take it. Lonely and terrified, and exhausted from the treatment, they would quietly withdraw from the academy.

Like most plebes, Jimmy spent his entire first year there scared and very homesick. Because of his southwest Georgia accent, he was constantly teased about being a hillbilly or a hick from the sticks or a hayseed. Yet he was absolutely determined to get through the year and go on, so he kept his feelings to himself. "It never entered my mind to quit," he said years later, "I mean, not once."

One evening a group of upperclassmen ordered him out of his room. Gathering round him, they ordered him to sing "Marching Through Georgia." Jimmy froze. It was a Civil War song sung by Yankee soldiers as they marched south, burning and pillaging everything around them. Even a hundred years later, its lyrics enraged all true-blue Southerners. Jimmy stared at the upperclassman who'd made the traitorous request, then shook his head from side to side. "No sir," he said, "I won't sing that one." And he did not, even though he knew that his refusal would bring him even worse hazing for the rest of that year.

Jimmy spent the next summer at sea. Although the country was engaged in warfare in both the Atlantic and the Pacific, Jimmy's first assignment as a midshipman was with a group of other Annapolis students aboard the USS *New York,* a creaking old battleship doing patrol duty up and down the East Coast and in the Caribbean.

Jimmy had two permanent jobs aboard, one that he liked and the other that he hated. The former was on deck, manning a battle station located at a forty-five-millimeter antiaircraft battery. His other job was to clean the "after head," the toilet in the rear of the ship. What made this job so loathsome was that the toilet consisted of two troughs that were attached to the walls of a wedge-shaped compartment with a constant flow of salt water running into them that washed human wastes into the sea. During rough weather, however, every bit of the muck in the troughs would slosh onto the floor. And, of course, it was up to Jimmy to clean it up!

The closest the *New York* came to action that summer was the day the ship detected what it thought might be a German submarine. At top speed it began zigzagging, frantically trying to escape the unseen enemy. Suddenly in the midst of these violent maneuvers, a blade from one of the ship's four huge screws broke off, causing it to lurch and shudder. Had it been hit by a German torpedo or had it merely run into a reef? No one knew. But long after the ship had limped back into port for repairs, everyone aboard, including Jimmy and the other young Annapolis midshipmen, were awarded combat ribbons.

Jimmy's second year at the academy was much better than his first. Freed from the constant hazing and torment that had filled his life as a plebe, he felt more relaxed and sure of himself. Because he had little difficulty with any of his subjects and plenty of free time, he began taking flight instruction at a nearby naval base, learning in time how to handle several different kinds of navy planes. Even though flight training was not something required or even suggested at Annapolis, Jimmy's nature made him want to explore beyond what he needed to know simply because the opportunity was available.

After a second cruise during the summer of 1945, Jimmy spent the final days before returning to Annapolis back home in Plains. Ordinarily the requirement for graduation from the academy entailed a four-year course of study. But because of the war, it had been shortened to three years, so Jimmy had only one more year to go.

Early one evening he and a friend were driving around Plains in an old rumble seat Ford. Cruising past the Plains Methodist Church, they spotted Jimmy's sister Ruth and her friend Rosalynn Smith. Jimmy had seen Rosalynn with Ruth at his house frequently in the past, but she was three years younger than he and, as he recalled later,

Jimmy sent this photograph to Rosalynn during his final year at Annapolis.

he had always dismissed her as "an insignificant little girl." Yet that night the two young men were bored, looking for something to do. So they casually asked Ruth and Rosalynn if they'd like to go to the movies in Americus.

Rosalynn Eleanor Smith was a pretty, eighteen-year-old brunette who, like Jimmy, had been born and raised in Plains. Unlike Jimmy, her family had had very little money. Her father, who had died when she was thirteen, had been a mechanic and her mother worked as a seamstress. As the oldest of four children, she had had to take on much of the responsibility for running the household and helping her mother after her father's death.

A good student with a quick, eager mind, Rosalynn had been the only one in her high school class to go to college. Then a sophomore at Georgia Southwestern, she had a strong ambition to leave Plains, move faraway from Sumter County, and see the world. Somehow, she felt, there had to be more to life than the block-long row of stores in Plains where men lazily congregated across the tracks at the service station, chewing tobacco and drinking soft drinks spiked with whiskey.

That night, when Jimmy came by to pick her up, he must have seemed everything she was looking for—a sophisticated Annapolis man who'd already seen and done things she could scarcely imagine. As Rosalynn's mother recalls, "He was really a good-looking fellow in that white uniform. And he had all those amazing teeth, so white, so white."

After the movies Jimmy asked Rosalynn for a "late date" the following night, his last night home. She hesitated, not sure whether it was proper for her to go out with him after he'd already delivered his regular date back to her house. But knowing that she wouldn't see him again till Christmas vacation, she couldn't resist.

All that fall Jimmy and Rosalynn wrote letters back and forth. At Christmas they saw each other every night. By then both were completely smitten. When Jimmy proposed to Rosalynn the night before Christmas, however, he was stunned by her answer. It was no. "I was so young," she recalls. "I hadn't made up my mind about much of anything yet—a career or anything, you know—and this was something I hadn't even thought about at all: getting married—and at my age. I wasn't about to make up my mind on something like that on the spur of the moment."

Recovering from his initial shock, Jimmy felt even more intrigued and challenged by this baffling young woman. The more he thought about her, the more he liked her hesitancy, the fact that she was not a girl for whom a marriage proposal was everything. From the academy that winter, he continued to court her. Knowing how much she longed to leave Plains, he wrote lengthy descriptions of the horizons that would open up to her as the wife of a naval officer, the ports they would visit, the places she could live, the experiences they would share. When she came up to Annapolis for the festive Washington's Birth-

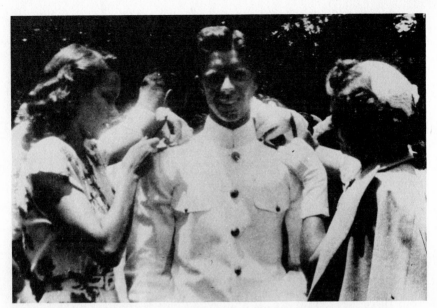

At his graduation from Annapolis, Jimmy gets his bars pinned on by his bride-to-be and his mother.

day weekend, he proposed again. This time she accepted.

In June 1946, Jimmy was graduated from the United States Naval Academy. He placed fifty-ninth in a graduating class of more than eight hundred men, which put him in the top 10 percent. At the graduation ceremonies, his future bride, Rosalynn, and his proud mother, Lillian, took their places on either side of him to snap the ensign's bars on his shoulders.

A few weeks later on the hot, sultry afternoon of July 7, 1946, Rosalynn and Jimmy were married in the Plains Methodist Church. She was not quite nineteen, he was twenty-one. Immediately after the ceremony, the newly-weds drove away from the little town they both called home. They began heading north to their new home together in Norfolk, Virginia, where Jimmy had been given his first assignment as an officer in the United States Navy.

4

Life in the U.S. Navy

The year 1946 was a difficult time to begin a career as a young officer in the U.S. Navy. World War II had just ended and the country was enjoying peace at last. The postwar navy was in poor shape, having less than half its wartime manpower. Additionally, more than two thousand ships had been deactivated and another seven thousand declared surplus.

Jimmy's first assignment, drawn purely by chance while he was still at Annapolis, was aboard a decrepit old battleship, the USS *Wyoming*, operating out of Norfolk, Virginia. The ship had been converted into a floating laboratory for testing experimental radar and new electronics and gunnery equipment. Jimmy, now Ensign Carter, was the officer in charge of the ship's electronics and photography, responsible for recording the accuracy of the new weapons. He was also the officer in charge of supervising the men aboard who'd enlisted at the high school and college level.

"The work was interesting," he said, "but the duty was terrible." Like so many ships operating after the war, the *Wyoming* was pitifully undermanned, creating twice as much work for those aboard. Also, the ship spent almost all of its time at sea so that the men seldom saw their loved ones.

Jimmy Carter of the United States Navy.

So, for the first two years of their marriage, Rosalynn spent most of her time alone in their tiny apartment in Norfolk. But she didn't mind. Life so far away from Plains became even more rewarding than she had expected. "I think we were as happy, individually and as a couple, as we possibly could have been. I know I was. It was hard, but ... I was growing and I knew it, and that really made me happy. I was finding out that I could do just about whatever I set out to do, which is a wonderful thing to know about yourself. ... I was handling our money and paying our bills and saving and scrimping and making do with what we had—and I know it was one of the most important periods in my life. I feel like I probably grew up in Norfolk or close to it." Adding to the couple's happiness was the birth of their son Jack the summer after their marriage. The baby was christened John William Carter after Rosalynn's grandfather.

Jimmy, meanwhile, decided that a solid future in the navy required a change from his present status, so he chose submarine service as his logical next step. Not only was it considered the most elite and dangerous branch of the navy, but it also offered the quickest way to promotion. Always ambitious, Jimmy even allowed himself to dream of one day becoming the navy's chief of operations.

So in the summer of 1948, he and Rosalynn and one-year-old Jack moved to New London, Connecticut, where Lieutenant Carter entered the navy's submarine school.

He loved it far more than anything he'd ever done at Annapolis. Each student had to learn thoroughly about each of the various systems aboard submarines—fuel, hydraulics, air pressure, fresh water, electricity, diesel engines, radar, fire control, torpedoes, gunnery, and sonar communications. There were long sessions on underwater strategy when students and instructors engaged in mock battles. New ideas and new questions confronted students every day. This was exactly the way Jimmy liked life—filled with challenges leading to new levels of achievement.

Completing submarine school that December, he and his family returned to Plains for the holidays. They didn't know when they'd next get back to Georgia. Jimmy had received his first submarine assignment and it was a prize. He was to be among the officers on the USS *Pomfret*, which meant that Rosalynn and Jimmy's new home would be in faraway Hawaii.

Leaving his wife and baby behind in Plains for a while, Jimmy reported aboard the *Pomfret* in January 1949. The sub embarked almost immediately for the coast of China where it was to serve as an underwater practice target for American and British crews aboard surface vessels.

On the voyage the young lieutenant barely escaped being lost at sea. The sub had run into a huge storm that lasted five days, making everyone very seasick. One night, after it had surfaced to recharge batteries, Jimmy climbed onto the bridge about fifteen feet above the water. Seemingly from nowhere, an enormous wave began to rise. It rose higher and higher, threatening to swallow the ship. When it was about six feet above Jimmy's head, its sheer force tore his hand from the railing. Suddenly he was completely separated from the submarine, swimming within the wave, water all around him. Then the wave receded, depositing Jimmy on the barrel of a gun located about thirty feet behind the sub's conning tower. Hanging on desperately, he finally managed to lower himself to the deck and onto the bridge again. It was pure luck that he was still alive. "Had the currents been even slightly broadside instead of from forward to aft," he said later, "I never would have landed on the ship."

Except for that close call, Jimmy loved his duty on the *Pomfret* and was convinced that it was the best vessel in the navy. That was exactly the way he should have felt, for pride is essential for men who spend long, lonely weeks living beneath the ocean's surface. On board a submarine, the key to living and operating successfully is interdependence, with each enlisted man being an expert in one area of responsibility, dependent on others to be equally skillful in their areas. As an officer, however, Jimmy had to know every aspect of the ship as well as every crew member's individual job.

A week after the *Pomfret* returned to Hawaii from China in April 1949, Rosalynn and Jack joined Jimmy. They settled into a comfortable two-bedroom apartment on the island of Oahu. With beautiful weather and the low cost of living, the Carters found Hawaii an idyllic assignment. In April 1950 their second son, James Earl Carter III, was born in Honolulu. The nurses at the hospital were so startled by the baby's striking resemblance to his father that they called him a "chip off the old block." The name stuck. Thereafter the new baby was always called Chip.

In the early summer of that year, America again found itself engaged in a war that started when North Korea invaded South Korea. Although Washington never called America's involvement "a war," but rather a "police action" against communism, the United States began bombing

North Korean troops and later sent in American ground troops. Because of Korea's inland location, however, the U.S. Navy was not involved.

The *Pomfret* was ordered back to San Diego, California, and that fall Jimmy got new orders. He was to be the senior officer on the navy's first postwar submarine, the USS *K-1*, an experimental vessel, not yet launched, that was to function as an antisubmarine or, as some people called it, a sub killer.

The Carters moved back to New London, where the *K-1* was nearing completion. As the navy's agent for the final installation of the sub's sophisticated equipment, Jimmy spent the first few months checking and rechecking equipment going aboard, and also planning testing procedures that would be followed when the ship was launched. After a shakedown cruise in the winter of 1951, Lieutenant Carter spent weeks at sea while the new sub practiced locating and disposing of other submarines. Later, when officers with more seniority were assigned to the *K-1* after it was launched, Jimmy became the junior officer in charge of the engineering division. He was also promoted to the rank of full lieutenant.

Meanwhile, Jimmy was again looking ahead. Convinced that atomic submarines would be the most important future area of the navy, he applied for what he believed was the best possible job available to someone of his rank—the atomic division of the Bureau of Ships, headed by Capt. Hyman G. Rickover. As a follow-up to his application, he was called to Washington to be interviewed by Rickover.

When they met, Carter was twenty-six and Rickover was fifty-one. A budding nuclear physicist and a passionate believer in the use of atomic submarines, Rickover had graduated at the top of his class at Annapolis in 1922 and had gone on to establish a widespread reputation as a brilliant officer with unequaled expertise in electrical engineering. Their first meeting had a lasting impact on the ambitious young lieutenant.

Lt. Jimmy Carter, standing rear, aboard the Navy's first postwar submarine, the U.S.S. "K-1."

The interview lasted more than two hours, with the two sitting alone in a large room. Rickover began by asking Jimmy to choose any subjects he wished to discuss. Carefully, Jimmy chose those things about which he felt he knew the most—current events, seamanship, music, literature, naval tactics, electronics, and gunnery. The interrogation was a disaster. Rickover sat stone-faced, staring straight into Jimmy's eyes, asking him increasingly difficult questions about each subject. Within short order, Rickover had proved that he knew so much more about every subject that it was as if Jimmy knew almost nothing. By then his body was saturated in cold sweat.

Finally Rickover took another line of questioning. "How did you stand in your class at the academy?" he asked.

At last, thought Jimmy, a question that would help redeem him in the captain's eyes. "Sir," he replied proudly,

"I stood fifty-ninth in a class of eight hundred and twenty!" He waited for Rickover to congratulate him.

But the captain remained unsmiling. "Did you do your best?"

Surprised, Jimmy started to reply, "Yes sir." But then he remembered that it was Hyman Rickover to whom he was talking and, yes, there had been times when he probably could have done better. So he quietly answered, "No sir, I didn't *always* do my best."

Rickover looked at him long and hard. "Why not?" he asked. Then, in a gesture of utter contempt, the captain turned his chair all the way around, to end the interview. Shaken, Carter remained seated a while. Then as if struggling to pull himself out of a nightmare, he slowly got up and left.

Despite Rickover's stern demeanor, he must have liked something about Jimmy, perhaps his honesty. For to Jimmy's amazement, he was offered the job. Thus, shortly after their third son, Donnel Jeffrey Carter, was born in New London, the family of five moved to Schenectady, New York. There Jimmy became the senior officer of a crew being assembled for the navy's new atomic submarine, the *Seawolf.*

One of Jimmy's duties was to teach a variety of subjects, such as reactor technology and physics, to the enlisted men in the crew, all handpicked by Rickover. To do this he had to take special graduate courses in the same subjects at nearby Union College. After learning something himself, he would then teach it to his men.

Frequently Rickover would show up in Schenectady to inspect his men's work. On these visits it seemed impossible to please the captain. If Jimmy had done a good job at something, Rickover never praised him but simply looked at what he was doing and walked away. "However," Jimmy remembers, "if I made the slightest mistake, in one of the loudest and most obnoxious voices I'd ever heard, he would turn around and tell people in the area what a horrible disgrace I was to the navy and that I ought to be back in the oldest and slowest submarine from which I'd come."

Yet Hyman Rickover was a hero of Jimmy's. Although he was afraid of him, he admired him more than any man he'd ever met and he picked up traits of Rickover's, making them a permanent part of his own character. "He always insisted that we know our jobs in the most minute detail, which is really a necessary, basic characteristic of a good submariner. Also," adds Jimmy, "he was unbelievably hardworking and competent, by any measure a remarkable man, probably the greatest naval engineer the nation ever produced."

Meanwhile Jimmy had received sad news from Plains. His father was dying of cancer. In the eleven years since he'd left home, a distance had grown between father and son, brought about, certainly, by the totally different things the two were doing. Then Jimmy began taking leaves to be home with his father. Talking about old times together and about all that had happened in the intervening years, they began to reestablish their former closeness.

Earl Carter died on July 22, 1953. After the funeral, stories about him began to be told that Jimmy had never heard—how for years he'd quietly bought graduation clothes for children in Plains who couldn't afford them; how he'd helped support a poor widow in town; how he'd lent money to the farmers who'd bought his seed and fertilizer. Yet Earl Carter's brand of charity was so quiet that even his own family had never been aware of all he'd done.

Moved by his father's deep commitment to family, friends, and neighbors, Jimmy suddenly begin to re-examine his own life. He thought about his naval career. He thought, too, of the business his father had worked so hard to build, of his widowed mother, of his fifteen-year-old brother, Billy, left without a male role model. In recent years, he discovered, his father's debts had mounted, leaving the family with little cash. What would happen to the farm and to the family he loved?

Jimmy began weighing the idea of coming home to Plains for good. And he began asking himself some hard questions. "Did I want to be the chief of naval operations and devote my whole life to that narrowly defined career, which was a good one? Or did I want to go back and build a more diverse life with a lot of friends, permanence, stability, in a community, in a relationship, in the life of a whole group of people?" It was a hard decision. But when he made it, he was firm in his resolve: he would come home to Plains.

After driving back to Schenectady, he told Rosalynn of his decision. She couldn't believe it. Go back to Plains, back to the heat and provincialism of Sumter County? She loved being a navy wife, the moving around, the new friends, their cosmopolitan life. She was furious. They had a bitter fight. But Jimmy was insistent.

Later that summer, as he and Rosalynn and their three little boys drove into Plains, he turned to her as she stared sullenly out the window and said cheerfully, "Welcome home!"

5

The Return to Plains

Settling down in Plains, Jimmy threw himself into farming with the same single-minded determination he'd used pursuing a career in the navy. He grilled everyone about the business and read all he could about the latest agricultural techniques. In partnership with his mother, he put nearly all the money he and Rosalynn had managed to save into buying farm equipment.

The work was hard and exhausting, often stretching into sixteen- and eighteen-hour days. There were two aspects to it: first, the farming—endless cycles of cultivating, planting, harvesting, and selling crops; Second, the merchandising—warehousing his and other farmers' crops as well as storing feed, seed, and fertilizer for customers. As luck would have it, his first year in business, 1954, coincided with one of the worst droughts in Georgia's history. All his crops were ruined and none of his customers could pay back the credit he had extended to them. Jimmy's total income that year was less than two hundred dollars.

To make matters worse, Rosalynn was miserably unhappy. Because of a housing shortage in Plains, she and

Jimmy moved into a government housing project for which they qualified because of their low income. Although the project housed nine other families, Rosalynn kept to herself, making slipcovers and curtains, cooking, cleaning, leading the life of a typical 1950's housewife. But that's what she hated. She didn't want to gossip across clotheslines, go to bridge parties, and drink too much coffee with the other women. No matter how many times Jimmy told her that one day she'd be glad they'd come back to Plains, she couldn't see it. "I will not ever be glad!" she would shout. "Don't say that anymore."

One afternoon in the spring of 1955, Jimmy phoned to see if she could relieve him at the office so he could get away to call on some customers. Because he'd had no money to hire help, he'd been doing everything—cleaning the office, buying and selling seed and fertilizer, loading it on the farmers' trucks, keeping the books, and making out bills. Rosalynn not only went that afternoon, taking the children with her, but she kept going. Initially she liked it because it got her out of the house. But later, after she'd become the full-time office manager, keeping books and paying bills, she became indispensible to the business and as responsible for its financial success as Jimmy was. Not only was he proud of her accounting skills, but he depended on her. Whereas they'd each grown in separate ways while he was in the navy, now they grew together. Their marriage flourished as never before.

With the drought of 1954 giving way to the rains of 1955, the mood of Plains turned from despair to jubilation. Tons of peanuts poured into the Carter's warehouse to be weighed, evaluated, and stored or shipped out of town and turned into a variety of peanut products. With more income, the family rented a big, rambling house outside of Plains where the boys had room for a horse as well as several dogs. Meanwhile Jimmy was as energetic as ever about the business. No sooner had they finished paying off what they owed for one piece of equipment than he'd

Jimmy stands atop a mountain of peanuts in his warehouse in Plains.

begin dreaming of something else he wanted to do. He was forever expanding, adding on, building, and experimenting.

Like his father, he also contributed his time to a long list of civic organizations. He became director of the county chamber of commerce, a member of the library board, the hospital authority, and the county school board. As project chairman of the Lions Club, he helped organize everyone in Plains to get together to improve the town. First the streets were paved, then people painted their houses, finally enough money was raised at bake sales and town picnics to build a community swimming pool. Bursting with pride, the people of Plains entered the town in the Better Home Towns Contest, coming away with two first prizes and two seconds.

Both Jimmy and Rosalynn were active in the doings at the Plains Baptist Church. As the leader of the Royal Ambassadors, a church club for young boys, Jimmy helped design and build a camp for the boys. Also he and Rosalynn, who had followed her husband into the Baptist church after their return to Plains, both taught Sunday School—at church on Sundays and at the Baptist Teaching Union at night.

It wasn't long before Jimmy's civic responsibilities had expanded beyond Plains and Sumter County. Each new job made him a little better known as a valued volunteer leader. He helped organize a seven-county planning commission; he became president of the Georgia Crop Association; he was selected state chairman for the March of Dimes. And he rose to the very top position in the Lions Club, becoming chairman of the state's district governors.

Life, however, was not all hard work and good causes. He and Rosalynn played golf, took dancing lessons, and signed up for a speed reading course at the college in Americus. With their sons, they went on frequent camping trips as well as on a fishing trip to Florida and to the automobile races in Sebring. The two traveled to Cuba one year and to New Orleans with friends another, where they stayed up all night, excited by the fabulous jazz and exotic food. By then Rosalynn was admitting that Jimmy had been right—it *was* good to be back in Plains.

But trouble was brewing in the South. It had started in 1954 when the U.S. Supreme Court had ruled that public schools could no longer be segregated. From then on, according to the ruling, black and white children would have to attend the same schools. Most white Southerners were horrified. Having grown up in a society where black people were forbidden to eat at restaurants that served white customers, or to sit next to a white person on a public bus, they were infuriated by a federal law requiring their children to mingle with black children in classrooms. If the law was obeyed, people speculated, there was no telling where it would lead. Intermarriage between the races? Yes, even that. And that possibility was enough to curdle the blood of most white Southerners.

Certainly Earl Carter, Jimmy's father, would have become furious even at the suggestion of racial integration. But Jimmy felt differently. As a boy, he had had black playmates and been strongly influenced by his mother's gentle concern for blacks. And having spent years traveling around the country while in the navy, both he and Rosalynn had come to believe that integration was inevitable. Considering themselves realists rather than liberals, they nonetheless avoided the topic when they were with most of their friends.

In response to the Supreme Court's ruling, Southern whites began establishing White Citizens Councils, organizations that vowed to fight furiously against integration. In 1958 a White Citizens Council was formed in Plains by some of the town's leading citizens. One day the police chief and one of the local preachers came to see Jimmy at work, asking him to join. He refused politely. They came again two days later, telling him that time that he was the only white man in Plains who hadn't become a member. Again he refused. So a week later they returned a third time, in a group that then included some of Jimmy's best friends and customers. Pointing out that his refusal to join would damage his reputation and his business success, they offered to pay the five-dollar membership for him. Jimmy was furious. No, he told them frostily, he was not going to join. Not ever. As to his being hurt financially, well then, so be it. He had moved before, and if he had to, he would move again.

The council tried to organize a boycott of Jimmy's business, which frightened the Carters. But the boycott didn't work. Although a couple of customers never came back, most people were too loyal to stay away for good.

By 1962 the race issue was more heated than ever. Jimmy's strongest civic concerns at that time were those he faced as a member of the county school board. Along with the majority of the board, he had concluded that the best way to improve the quality of education at the high school level was to consolidate the three existing high schools, each one inadequate by itself, into one large school that could offer a wide range of courses and activities. But the county's citizens were opposed to the idea. Not only did they oppose the loss of hometown schools, but a few of the more vocal opponents argued that the change would play into Washington's avowed goal of getting blacks and whites in school together. Although Jimmy spoke on behalf of the consolidation plan, the issue was continually defeated when it was brought to a vote.

To ease people's worst fears about future integration — the fear of boys and girls of the two races mingling and possibly dating — the school board proposed another plan: two schools, one for girls and one for boys. Again Jimmy argued strenuously for the new plan. The vote took place just before he and Rosalynn went to a basketball game in which their son Jack was playing. When the announcement came during a break that once again the school plans had been defeated, the audience broke into joyful cheering. The Carters sat quietly, depressed by the news. After the game they walked home. As they passed their office, they noticed a hand-scrawled note tacked to the office door. It read: Coons and Carters Go Together. Sickened by the hatred in the message, they ripped the sign down.

But Jimmy was not one to retreat meekly. Having had a taste of local politics, he was intrigued by the political process. Awakening the morning of his thirty-eighth birthday, he announced to Rosalynn that he had decided to run for the Georgia State Senate.

6

Jimmy Who?

Jimmy Carter's first foray into the world of politics was an eye-opener. Yet running for office was not new to the Carters. Jimmy's father had died while serving as a state representative. Since returning to Plains, Jimmy occasionally had considered entering state politics too, but until recently there had been little opportunity. As a resident of Sumter County, he was part of a three-county election district in which candidates were traditionally handpicked by a small group of political bosses.

But that situation changed in the early 1960s. To comply with the recent U.S. Supreme Court ruling of "one man, one vote," Jimmy's district had been expanded to include seven counties. A special election had been called, and for the first time in memory, the race was wide open. Jimmy felt he had a good chance. Not only was he from the largest county in the new district but, because of his widespread business dealings, he was known by most of the farmers in the area.

With only two weeks before the primary, Jimmy, Rosalynn, Jimmy's sister Ruth, and several close friends mounted what the candidate later affectionately called "an amateurish, whirlwind campaign." While Rosalynn tended the warehouse, Jimmy took to the road, visiting every village in every county, shaking thousands of hands, working

Flashing his famous grin, Jimmy shook thousands of hands in the 1962 Georgia State Senate race.

much harder than his opponent. Rosalynn and the others, meanwhile, spent their spare time phoning and writing to hundreds of names on the voting lists.

Leaving nothing to chance, Jimmy spent primary day going from one county polling place to the next to greet voters. When he got to Quitman County, however, he could hardly believe what he saw. Instead of the usual polling booths, all the voters were marking their ballots in public while the county boss, Joe Hurst, looked on. Jimmy strongly protested, but no one paid any attention to him. Clearly this was the way Joe Hurst had always run elections in his county and he intended to keep on running them this way.

That night, after the vote had come in from every county except Quitman, Jimmy was leading. Then came the Quitman vote, and it was a strange one. Although only 330 people had been recorded as having voted, 430 votes were tabulated — enough to carry Jimmy's opponent to victory in the overall primary. Jimmy instantly challenged the results. To get proof of election fraud, he began going back to Quitman County each day to collect affidavits from voters. He noticed that two strange men always followed him, standing quietly in the background and recording on note pads everything he did. Apparently Joe Hurst did not like his authority in Quitman County being questioned.

In the six remaining weeks before the general election there were court hearings, appeals, and counterappeals. At first no one could find the Quitman County ballot box. Finally it was discovered under the bed of Joe Hurst's daughter. But when it was opened in court and neither the voting list nor any of the ballots were in it, a neutral judge declared Jimmy the winner of the primary. But then the local Democratic Executive Committee, controlled by Joe Hurst, stepped in and overturned the judge's decision. Jimmy's opponent was again declared the winner.

The election mess in southwest Georgia by then had attracted statewide attention. One of Atlanta's most prominent lawyers, Charles Kirbo, persuaded Georgia's secretary of state to issue a last-minute order that Jimmy's name be substituted for his opponent's on the election ballots. The problem was time. Jimmy and his family and all of their friends had to stay up most of the night on election eve handstamping Jimmy's name onto all of the ballots in all seven courthouses. When the news finally

Jimmy, top right, is sworn in to the Georgia State Senate.

came the next night that Jimmy had won the seat for state senator by 851 votes, he and his small band of loyal campaign aides were too exhausted to feel much jubilation. Besides, they were all a bit sickened by their first brush with politics.

Nor were the Carters through with Joe Hurst. As soon as Jimmy left for the legislative session in Atlanta in early 1963, Rosalynn got a message from Mr. Hurst that the last time he had been crossed, the person's liquor store had burned down. Rosalynn knew it was no idle threat. She knew about a liquor store that had burned to the ground, a legal liquor business that had been in direct competition with Joe Hurst's illegal moonshine operation.

Legislative sessions lasted about two and a half months each year in Atlanta. All the time Jimmy was away that first year, Rosalynn lived in terror. Would their warehouses and house meet the same fate as that liquor store had? Afraid to leave the boys in the house alone, she had them meet her at the warehouse after school. And every night when they all got home, she would check quickly under the beds to be sure no one was hiding. When it was time for bed, she left the porch and hall lights on and barricaded the doors with chairs. Fortunately nothing happened. By the time Jimmy departed for his second legislative session, Rosalynn's fear had subsided.

Winning reelection in 1964, Jimmy served in the Georgia senate for a total of four years. Seldom absent from sessions, he amazed other legislators by the thorough homework he had done on each of the more than one thousand bills that reached the senate floor. In addition to being noted for his strong interest in public education and his keen dislike for lobbyists, he served on the senate's appropriations committee, becoming an expert on taxes and a critic of the disorganization he saw in the state government. Although he helped repeal Georgia's infamous "30 questions," a voting test meant to keep blacks from voting, he managed to keep his views on racial issues rather quiet. To his constituents in southwest Georgia, that was just fine. The last thing they wanted was a representative who would push integration.

By 1964 the race issue had turned the traditionally Democratic South into a stronghold for Barry Goldwater, the conservative Republican presidential candidate. Among the Democrats, only Governor George Wallace of Alabama, an arch segregationist, was a hero. But Jimmy and his family felt differently from the majority of Southern Democrats. Not only did they dislike Wallace, but they strongly supported the Democratic presidential candidate, Lyndon Johnson. Jimmy's mother, Lillian, who had recently returned after seven years as a housemother at a fraternity house at the University of Alabama, actually ran Johnson's headquarters in Americus. Because Johnson was deemed a liberal on race issues, she would often find her car after work smeared with soap or the car's antenna tied in a knot.

By then the race issue had reached the boiling point locally. A white teenager had been killed by blacks in Americus. When the Plains Baptist Church voted on whether to admit blacks, the only members of the congregation to vote for it were the Carters. This was enough to arouse suspicion among a few of the more rabid segregationists in town. When Jimmy and Rosalynn took their sons on a vacation to Mexico during the summer of 1965, a rumor was spread that they were at a camp run by Communists in Alabama that trained integration workers. When they returned to Plains and no customers appeared at their warehouse, Jimmy and Rosalynn had to spend several days convincing people where they'd really been.

While all of this was going on, Jimmy was beginning to think increasingly about his political future. When Barry Goldwater won the state of Georgia in his 1964 presidential race, he had carried with him a few other Republican candidates. One of them was the winner of the U.S. congressional race in Jimmy's district, Howard "Bo" Callaway, a man Jimmy disliked intensely. The heir to a textile fortune, Callaway had become the first Republican from Georgia to serve in Congress since the Civil War. Quietly Jimmy began making plans to challenge him in 1966.

In some ways the two were well-paired competitors. Like Jimmy, Bo had also sought a career in the military, graduating from the U.S. Military Academy at West Point. Like Jimmy, Bo had given up a promising military career to return to Georgia to build his father's business. But unlike Jimmy, Bo was a millionaire for whom life had always been easy, and Jimmy resented that. Moreover, when Jimmy had tried successfully as a state senator to expand Georgia Southwestern in Americus from a junior college to a four-year college, Callaway, then a member of the state board of regents, had tried to block the move. Jimmy had never forgiven him.

By then it had become clear to everyone close to him that politics, not farming, had become Jimmy's whole life. In the spring of 1966, he formally announced his candidacy for the Democratic nomination to Congress. The long days on the road began again. And again, he gave hundreds of speeches and shook thousands of hands. But late that spring Bo Callaway abruptly withdrew from the race, announcing that he had decided to run for governor instead. Jimmy was stunned. Although Callaway had been the odds-on favorite for Congress, Jimmy had relished the idea of opposing him. With Callaway out of the picture, however, it looked as if Jimmy would be a shoo-in for Congress.

But what Democrat would give Callaway the best fight for the governorship? Opposing him were two well-known figures in the state. The first was Ellis Arnall, who had been governor twenty years earlier. Although he was considered honest and effective, many saw him as being out of touch with modern state government. The other was Lester Maddox, a die-hard segregationist who had become something of a folk hero to many Georgians for his fiery stance against integration. Horrified by the thought of Maddox walking away with the Democratic nomination, Charles Kirbo and several other influential Democrats approached Jimmy about running for governor. It was a tough decision. If he were to run for governor, he'd be throwing away a sure seat in the U.S. Congress. And for what? With only three months before the primary, he was completely unknown to the vast majority of voters outside his own district.

Still, the thought of beating Maddox and challenging Callaway proved irresistible, so Jimmy switched in midstream from being a U.S. congressional candidate to being a candidate for the Democratic nominee for governor. When news of his candidacy was announced, people across the state looked at each other in bewilderment. "Jimmy Who?" they asked.

In a frantic effort to make up for their late entry into the primary, the Carters launched their first all-family campaign. While Billy Carter and his wife, Sybil, ran the warehouse, Jimmy, Jack, Chip, Lillian, and Rosalynn (with fourteen-year-old Jeff at her side) set out on separate routes and schedules across the state. In borrowed cars with posters of Jimmy taped to the sides, they drove through every town in Georgia, introducing themselves along the way. Few people had even heard of Jimmy. But that didn't matter. The family kept going. By primary day Jimmy's standing in the public opinion polls had risen dramatically. But not enough.

Jimmy lost the primary to both his competitors, Arnall and Maddox, by twenty thousand votes out of a million cast. What followed was a lesson in how elections can go wrong. Since neither Arnall nor Maddox won a clear majority in the primary, there was a runoff. Maddox won because many Republicans crossed over to vote for him, thinking he'd be the easiest for Callaway to beat in the general election. When that election occurred, however, there was such a large write-in vote from Georgians unwilling to support either Callaway or Maddox that no one won a majority. Thus the state legislature was required by law to choose a winner. Consisting largely of conservative Democrats in 1966, the legislature declared Lester Maddox, the arch-segregationist, as Georgia's new governor.

The morning after his primary defeat, Jimmy gathered his family and supporters around him and announced that he planned a second run for governor in 1970. With steely determination in his pale blue eyes, he added, "I don't intend to lose again." Then he and his family went home to Plains.

The months that followed were depressing for Jimmy. Because of the campaign, he was sixty-six thousand dollars in debt and had lost twenty-two pounds. Moreover, he had given up a safe seat in the state senate, lost a really good chance to be in the U.S. Congress, and still hadn't been able to engage Bo Callaway in a head-on fight. He saw himself as having taken a giant slide backward to where he had been in 1962. Now, however, it was worse. Now that he was passionately caught up in politics, he was a candidate without an office.

While feeling so badly about himself, Jimmy had an experience that would later be questioned by millions of people during his future presidential campaign. He became a born-again Christian. It happened quite simply. One day he was on a walk with his sister Ruth, who was visiting from North Carolina. In searching for answers to her life, Ruth had turned more deeply to religion. Knowing this, Jimmy admitted to her that despite being a faithful churchgoer he wasn't as committed to his faith as he felt he should be. Recently, though, he told her, he had heard a sermon at church entitled, "If You Were Arrested for Being a Christian, Would There Be Any Evidence to Convict You?" They talked about the sermon, and they talked some more. As Ruth spoke about her own unshakable religious commitment, tears came to Jimmy's eyes and something deep inside him happened. From that moment on, he explained later, "I formed a much more intimate relationship with Christ."

In addition to the joy he then felt in his religion, there were other reasons why his depression lifted. After years of trying to have another child, Rosalynn gave birth in October 1967 to their first daughter, Amy. It seemed a miracle. When the three boys, then teenagers, saw their little sister, they were so excited that they burst into tears.

Meanwhile, though still an unannounced candidate, Jimmy was becoming more engaged by his second try for the governorship. "On a typical day, I would go to the warehouse or to the farm very early and work until sometime in the afternoon. Then I would drive somewhere in Georgia to make a speech and return home late at night. Names, information about the community, and speech notes were all dictated into a small tape recorder in the automobile. The next day Rosalynn wrote thank-you notes on the automatic typewriter, which also recorded names, addresses, and code descriptions of the persons I had met."

When he was alone, Jimmy spent hours studying issues and reading books on the environment, education, health care, crime control, and the criminal justice system. Dozens of young people who had volunteered for him before joined the effort and Jimmy asked some of them to prepare detailed analyses of every Georgia election in the past twenty years. By 1968 he had begun to understand something he had not fully grasped earlier: that Georgians were more conservative than he was on almost every single issue. It was a fact he could not afford to forget.

In late 1969, after it had become clear that Carl Sanders, another ex-governor, would be his strongest competition for the Democratic nomination, Jimmy commissioned a poll to determine his standing. The poll indicated that both Sanders and Carter were seen as liberals. It also indicated, however, that voters knew Sanders better and were more familiar with his political views. This was seen as an asset for Jimmy because, by emphasizing his moderate conservatism in relation to that of Sanders, he could play to the majority voters' bent toward conservatism.

Jimmy formally announced his second candidacy for governor on April 3, 1970. His platform was a model of political blandness, including promises "to serve all Georgians, not just a powerful few," "to make appointments on the basis of qualifications for the job and never for political expediency," and "to strengthen local government and return the control of all aspects of government to the people." The platform did the job of canceling Jimmy's former liberal image. In its place were the views of a candidate completely in step with most other white Georgians—a man who fiercely resented the federal government's attempts to change the way things had been in Georgia for so long.

Jimmy's new image had its rewards. Georgia's most conservative political leaders began falling in behind him, figuring that he was more to their liking than the liberal Carl Sanders. People who had warmed to Jimmy in his earlier campaigns couldn't quite believe it when they heard him publicly praise Lester Maddox as "the embodiment of the Democratic party" or promise, if elected, to invite the ferociously segregationalist governor of Alabama, George Wallace, to Georgia to discuss mutual problems. Most of his earlier supporters, however, forgave him. If a person wanted to be elected in the South at that time, he had to be in tune with the thinking of most of the voters.

The primary again ended in a runoff, this time between Sanders and Carter. Jimmy won the runoff and then went on to beat his Republican opponent, Hal Suit, in the general election. On November 2, 1970, seventeen years after he and Rosalynn had returned home to Plains, Jimmy Who? became the governor-elect of Georgia.

7

The Governor's Mansion and Beyond

When Jimmy Carter became the sixty-seventh governor of Georgia in January 1971, he gave an inaugural speech that surprised just about everyone. As he spoke, the faces of the die-hard segregationists who had supported his candidacy turned from puzzlement to outright dismay. " ... I realize the test of a man is not how well he campaigned," Jimmy began, as if backing away from the questionable campaign he had waged. Then he went on: "At the end of a long campaign, I believe I know our people as well as anyone. Based on this knowledge of Georgians—north and south, rural and urban, liberal and conservative—I say to you quite frankly that the time for racial discrimination is over."

The speech was only nine minutes long, but it was probably the most important speech of his life. Instantly it erased the very conservative, slightly racist image he'd projected in his 1970 campaign and restored the more moderate image he'd had during his unsuccessful 1966 race. National observers of the political scene took notice. The day after he was inaugurated, his speech was front-page news in the *New York Times*. A few weeks later his face beamed from the cover of *Time* magazine. Suddenly he had become one of the South's hopeful new voices, a symbol for an entire region that was changing.

Meanwhile, Jimmy and his family moved into Atlanta's Governor's Mansion. A lovely, massive house built in the classical style with columns on four sides, it sat on eighteen acres of lush lawns and gardens, completely surrounded by a tall wrought-iron fence. With a staff of servants to tend to their every need and the constant presence of state patrolmen to assure their security, their lives changed dramatically.

Now they were public figures living in a museum-like house. Four days a week groups of guided tourists streamed through it. As Georgia's foremost family, they were expected to entertain constantly. And they did, presiding over formal dinners for four hundred guests in the mansion's ballroom, or greeting people at gala receptions, luncheons, and barbecues. Among the varied groups invited to the mansion were governors of other Southern states, important people from Washington, corporate executives, legislative committees, county commissioners, mayors throughout Georgia, and many ordinary citizens.

Jimmy was a hardworking, effective, and innovative governor. The primary and immense task that he set for himself was reorganizing the state government, something that had not been done since the 1930s. He assembled a team of a hundred people from Georgia's largest businesses to study the maze of state agencies, bureaus, and commissions and to recommend ways to make the government work more efficiently and economically. This led to a dramatic decrease in the number of state agencies from three hundred to twenty-two.

Under his administration, the phrase "zero-based budgeting" became a familiar term in Georgia. This was a new fiscal arrangement under which all government departments that had, in the past, grown accustomed to asking

Jimmy Carter becomes governor of Georgia, switching the nameplates with Lester Maddox, the former governor, in the governor's office in the capitol at Atlanta.

for and automatically receiving yearly increases in funding, now had to reevaluate and justify each of their budget requests. Thus many state programs were either changed or eliminated, saving the state millions of dollars.

Insisting that all state jobs throughout the government be made available to black citizens, Carter increased the number of black state employees from 4,850 to 6,684. To defuse racial confrontation that had led to violence between blacks and whites in the past, he formed the Civil Disorder Unit, a biracial group trained to enter communities where tensions between blacks and whites were brewing and mediate the problems before they became worse.

Some people in Georgia, of course, didn't like Jimmy. They didn't like his sweeping changes. This was especially true within the conservative state legislature. Some of its members felt that Jimmy was scornful of all legislators and so determined to get his own bills passed that he was unwilling to compromise. One veteran of the legislative wars during this time had this to say: "Like a south Georgia turtle, that's what he's like. He just keeps on moving in the direction he's headed and it doesn't matter what you do to him. You can step on him or hit him with a stick or run over him with a pickup truck, and it doesn't faze him a bit. He just keeps right on going in the way he wants."

By 1972, only two years after becoming governor, it was clear that the place Jimmy wanted to go next was the White House. Under Georgia law, no governor was allowed to hold the governor's office for two four-year terms in a row. But how did he make the giant leap in his own mind from being a one-term state governor, completely unknown to most people outside Georgia, to being president of the United States?

Jimmy, himself, is vague: "I think it just evolved, probably without my being aware of it at all, until at some point or another I entertained the idea, probably for just a split second and probably without realizing I had. And then it probably occurred again, this time maybe for a little longer than the first, and also probably without my actual conscious realization that it was there until, finally, when I acknowledged that it was there, I couldn't remember when it wasn't there."

Certainly his competitive nature had something to do with the decision. In high school he had competed for grades with his girlfriend, Eloise Ratliff. When he had run for office in 1966, he was spurred on by his feelings of competitiveness with Bo Callaway. Now that he was governor, he was meeting the real stars of the Democratic party, men like Senators Kennedy, Muskie, McGovern, and Hubert Humphrey, men known from coast to coast. These meetings were bound to lead to comparisons. In fact, one night after entertaining one of these prominent Democrats, Rosalynn had said to him, "The boys and I think you'd be just as good a president as the senator, and probably much better."

Carter had laughed. "You and the boys are probably right," he had said, "but we'll have to get Amy's opinion."

No one can run for president without a loyal staff of supporters. And Jimmy had those. They were fellow Georgians, some of whom had been behind him since he'd first entered politics. Perhaps the one who supported him the longest, outside of his immediate family and friends, was Charles Kirbo, the influential lawyer who had paved Jimmy's way into the state senate in 1962. Others included Stuart Eisenstat, a young Atlanta attorney who had organized volunteers to analyze issues for the 1970 campaign; Frank Moore, who had worked with Jimmy on their local regional planning commission; Jerry Rafshoon, who had handled the advertising for his gubernatorial race; and Bert Lance, a robust banker from rural Georgia whom Jimmy had brought in to overhaul the state's department of transportation. But the man Jimmy felt personally closest to was Jody Powell, also a farmer's son from southwest Georgia, who had become his driver and adviser in the relentless search for votes during the 1970 campaign. On becoming governor, Jimmy had made Jody his press secretary.

Among all his supporters and aides, however, there wasn't anyone more important than Hamilton Jordan. The two had met in 1966 when Jordan became Jimmy's student coordinator. Then he had handled Jimmy's campaign strategy and scheduling in 1970 and from there had become the new governor's executive secretary in Atlanta.

In the spring of 1972 Jordan mentioned that possibly Jimmy should put forth his name to George McGovern as a vice presidential candidate. Jimmy liked the idea, but McGovern was opposed to it, so nothing happened. Immediately following the 1972 Democratic convention, Jordan wrote a detailed memo outlining what would have to occur for Carter to win the Democratic presidential nomination in 1976. The challenge was irresistible to Jimmy. From then on the possibility of becoming the next president was in his mind every time he gave a speech or traveled anywhere outside Georgia.

In 1973 Governor Carter became a member of the Trilateral Commission which had been organized by David Rockefeller, the powerful chairman of the Chase Manhattan Bank in New York. Its other members were impressive leaders on both sides of the Atlantic under the chairmanship of Dr. Zbigniew Brzezinski, a professor at Columbia University. Its purpose was to influence the foreign policy of all countries represented in its membership and to prevent further deterioration to the economic conditions between the United States, Japan, and non-Communist Europe. Carter was invited to join because he was seen as a representative of the "new" South. "A splendid learning experience," he said of his membership. But it was more than that—far more. Since he'd never had any experience in foreign policy, it gave him credentials as a knowledgeable leader of world affairs. And that, he knew, was vitally important for any presidential candidate.

Another helpful position came a year later, this one totally political. Robert Strauss, chairman of the Democratic National Committee, named him chairman of the 1974 Democratic campaign. Traditionally this was considered a tiresome and thankless job. But in Jimmy's case, it perfectly suited his presidential ambitions because it meant lots of travel, fund-raising speeches, and increased exposure. Even better, Strauss suggested that Carter bring Hamilton Jordan to Washington to work at the committee's headquarters for a while. Thus, while Jimmy was on the road giving Democrats a reason to remember him, Jordan was in Washington, learning how national campaigns were run.

Ever since Jimmy's inaugural speech as Georgia's new governor, he had become increasingly popular with black leaders. This was important too, for no Southerner could hope to win a presidential election without massive black support. At this time Jimmy approached Andrew Young, U.S. Congressman from Georgia since 1972, asking him to support his presidential quest. Young was no ordinary black leader. Having been the first black from the Deep South in nearly one hundred years to win a seat in Congress, he was a symbol of pride and hope to every black person in the nation. Although he knew he had a great deal to lose by backing a hopeless candidate—and an unknown ex-peanut farmer from Georgia hardly seemed a likely winner—he decided to throw his weight behind Jimmy.

At first it was thought the best time for Jimmy to announce his 1976 presidential candidacy would be in mid-1975. But in August 1974 President Nixon resigned under pressure and Jerry Ford became president. The day after Nixon's resignation, Jimmy telephoned Morris Dees, a handsome young millionaire and a liberal from Alabama, who had had remarkable success raising funds for George McGovern's 1972 presidential campaign. When Jimmy asked Dees to raise funds for him, Dees agreed. "I didn't know if he could win or not," said Dees, "but I didn't know anybody else who could either.... Besides, I was glad to see a Southerner besides George Wallace get into it."

Finally, on December 12, 1974, Jimmy publicly announced his candidacy. As he stood before a group of seasoned journalists inside Washington's National Press Club—a slight figure with a wide, engaging grin—the men and women of the press yawned and chuckled among themselves. Jimmy Carter, a presidential candidate? It seemed absurd. How many people in the country had even heard of him?

Jimmy said just about everything in his announcement speech that he would say in the long campaign ahead. He promised tax reform and welfare reform. He spoke of the need for a strong national defense and a more open government and greater privacy for the individual. He said there was a crisis in the public's confidence in government, that people needed a president they could believe in. "I'll never lie to you," he promised earnestly.

As he neared the end of his speech, his voice grew quieter. "It is now time to stop and to ask ourselves the question which my last commanding officer, Admiral Hyman Rickover, asked me and every other young naval officer who serves or has served in an atomic submarine." He paused, his light blue eyes searching the faces of his audience. "For our nation, for all of us, that question is 'Why not the best?'"

8

Racing Toward The White House

"Hello there. I'm Jimmy Carter."

"What did you say your name is?"

"Jimmy Carter, and I'm running for president."

"President of what?"

"President of the United States."

"Really? Come on, you gotta be joking!"

The reaction was always the same in those early days of the campaign: blank stares, astonishment, then gleeful delight. This nobody had the nerve to run for president? Well, either he must be a hopeless dreamer or, more likely, some kind of kook!

It has been said frequently that the most remarkable thing about Carter as president was that he ever got there at all. He had none of the attributes traditionally deemed necessary to run for president. Even after four years as governor of Georgia, only 2 percent of the voters in the nation had ever heard of him. Moreover, he not only had had no experience in Washington, but he had no close friends there in high places. Having never been appointed to a cabinet position and having never served in Congress, he came with no voting record whatsoever that might have reflected his position on important national issues.

So, who *was* he? About all that most people could say at first was that he was an ex-governor, a former farmer, and a man who claimed to be a born-again Christian, a term even most Christians found troubling. In addition to all his other problems, Jimmy Carter was a Southerner. And there hadn't been a U.S. president from the Deep South in more than a century.

But from the beginning, Jimmy and his campaign aides had seen these drawbacks as advantages. The country was fed up with politics-as-usual, distrustful of the people who ran the government from Washington. They had seen these high-and-mighty politicians paraded like common criminals across their television screens after the break-in of Democratic headquarters inside Washington's Watergate apartment complex. They had seen Richard Nixon resign the presidency in disgrace. And many people had been appalled when one of the first presidential acts of Jerry Ford was to pardon ex-President Nixon. Besides, what had these men with all their experience in Washington given the nation? Nothing! The United States had been badly wounded abroad by an ill-advised war in Vietnam. At home, soaring inflation was beginning to strangle many American families.

Thus the thrust of Jimmy's campaign was born. He would be a populist candidate, a man 'of the people' rather than a man from Washington. Instead of arguing issues, he would emphasize his personality. Taking strong stands on issues, after all, was the kind of thing that could abort a presidential candidacy. So he would offer broadly phrased opinions open to wide interpretation. For as he said, "I think our people have been hurt and scarred so badly by Vietnam, Cambodia, Watergate, the CIA revelations that they're just simply looking for somebody they can trust."

The long, grueling campaign on the road began in the early spring of 1975. It lasted for the next eighteen months during which Jimmy traveled five hundred thousand miles. Like his race for the governor, it was an all-family affair.

Only then, with all three Carter sons married, the family had grown to include their wives and even a small grandson. From Florida to Iowa to New Hampshire to Texas and back again to Iowa they trekked, pumping hands, raising money to keep going, giving speeches, appearing on radio talk shows, seeking press coverage and trying, above all, to give people reasons to remember Jimmy. Like the early Georgia campaigns, they carefully kept lists of people they'd met and wrote thousands of personal thank-you notes. Also, whenever possible, they stayed overnight in ordinary citizens' houses, which not only saved the cost of hotel rooms, but reinforced Jimmy's image as a man of the people.

It was an uphill struggle. The odds were against Jimmy. By December 1975, only seven months before the Democratic convention, the polls showed that he was the choice of less than 4 percent of Democrats. Meanwhile more and more contenders were entering the race for the Democratic nomination. The list ultimately included Morris Udall, George Wallace, Frank Church, Henry Jackson, Birch Bayh, Sargent Shriver, Jerry Brown, Ellen McCormack, Lloyd Bentsen, Milton Shapp, Terry Sanford, and Fred Harris—distinguished Democrats, most of them, with years of experience before the public eye. But unlike most of his competitors, who were currently serving as U.S. senators or state governors, Jimmy had no other job than the campaign itself, which meant he could run harder and longer than anyone else. Nor, perhaps, did any other Democratic contender want to be the next president as badly as Jimmy, nor have a wife and family who so wholeheartedly shared his ambition.

From the beginning, Carter and Hamilton Jordan had seen the importance of the state of Iowa in their overall campaign strategy. The very first Democratic state caucuses would be held there, preceding all of the state primaries. If Jimmy could do well among the local Democratic officials voting in these caucuses, it would have enormous publicity value. It would show Democrats everywhere that this 'nobody from Georgia' could be a winner. So, Jimmy and Rosalynn and their campaign aides visited Iowa time and time again.

Their strategy was correct and clever. The Iowa caucuses took place on January 19, 1976, and Jimmy's victory was big. He won 27 percent of the vote, while the runner-up, Senator Birch Bayh, pulled only 13 percent. The next morning Jimmy's name was on the front page of every newspaper in the country. People everywhere were amazed. Campaign donations began coming in and the phones in Carter's newly opened state headquarters began ringing with people volunteering to help. In politics, everyone likes a winner.

The New Hampshire primary, the first in the nation, took place a month later. Here, too, the Carter organization had been busy for months. Shortly after Christmas, Jeff Carter and his wife, Annette, moved into an apartment in the state to work full-time. About a month before the primary, nearly a hundred Georgians, calling themselves the Peanut Brigade, spent a week going door-to-door throughout New Hampshire, speaking to registered Democrats about Jimmy.

But the most important figure in the months before that primary had been Jimmy himself. As a campaigner, he was particularly effective when speaking before small gatherings of people, such as those at town meetings or parents/teachers groups. Fixing his clear blue eyes on the faces of his audience, he presented himself as an unusually bright and honest man, a man full of integrity. His words were often moving, such as the time he said to a group of New Hampshire schoolchildren, "If we could just have a government as good and as honest and as decent and as competent and as compassionate and as filled with love as are the American people, that would be a wonderful thing. And I believe we can, don't you?"

Jimmy greets a big crowd in Youngstown, Ohio, in quest of votes in that state's primary.

Perhaps more than anything, though, it was Jimmy's uniqueness that appealed to people and gave them such hope. When he quoted the noted theologian, Reinhold Niebuhr, college professors and graduate students in his audiences were stunned by the breadth of his knowledge. When he reeled off the lyrics of the folk singer, Bob Dylan, young people were delighted. When he spoke about national issues, he appealed to both conservatives and liberals, expressing the need for a strong military, less government spending, and more compassion for the poor and the helpless. Perhaps, thought many of the voters in New Hampshire, they didn't really know a lot about Jimmy Carter, but at least he offered freshness, a new vision of America—something more than politics-as-usual.

Jimmy won the New Hampshire primary with 30 percent of the vote. The Carter organization was elated. With two important victories, it looked as if Jimmy was on a roll. The important thing was to keep the momentum going.

The countdown of state primaries began. In March, despite a devastating loss in Massachusetts, where he'd spent little time campaigning, he defeated George Wallace in Florida. By the end of April, he'd added Illinois, North Carolina, and Wisconsin to his list of victories, and he'd also disposed of Henry Jackson in Pennsylvania. More and more Democratic candidates began dropping onto the sidelines. But the race wasn't over yet. In May he swept Texas, Georgia, and Indiana, but he lost Alabama, Nebraska, Maryland, Oregon, Idaho, and Nevada. Still ahead were the final primaries in early June, involving three big states—California, New Jersey, and Ohio.

He lost in both California and New Jersey, but his win in Ohio gave him a total of 1,260 of the 1,505 delegates he needed to secure the nomination. For the remaining candidates, the handwriting was all too clear. One by one, they began phoning Jimmy to pledge their delegates, and by mid-June he had won the nomination. It had been one of the fastest climbs from obscurity to victory in the history of presidential politics. How had it happened? people asked. Perhaps Patrick Cadell, Jimmy's pollster, said it best: "Jimmy was a stranger in town. They [the voters] had no reason to distrust him, and he didn't give them one."

The 1976 Democratic convention was held in the sweltering heat of New York City in mid-July. As delegates arrived from all over the country, they knew they would be part of a temporarily unified party whose presidential candidate had already emerged. Only one surprise lay ahead. Who would Jimmy Carter select for his running mate? Under intense press coverage, he had been interviewing a string of prominent Democrats for the past month. No one knew Jimmy's final choice, not even Rosalynn, until he announced it at the convention. The man he tapped to run for vice president turned out to be Walter "Fritz" Mondale.

Jimmy and his running mate, Walter ("Fritz") Mondale

It had been a difficult decision. But during their three-hour meeting in Plains, the two got along well and agreed on a variety of foreign and domestic issues. Politically, too, Mondale made sense. Not only was he a Washington "insider," which strengthened the ticket because of Jimmy's lack of experience there, but also he was from a part of the country that was geographically advantageous. As a Minnesotan, Mondale had strong midwestern support as well as the support of Hubert Humphrey's followers in the party.

By Labor Day, Jimmy and his family were back on the road, this time campaigning against the incumbent Republican president, Gerald Ford. The race was close. Following the Republican convention in August, Jimmy's lead had plummeted from a high of twenty-five points to eight or nine. He hoped that the three nationally televised debates between President Ford and himself, which would be the first presidential debates since John F. Kennedy had sparred with Richard Nixon in 1960, would reassure people about his qualifications. It is commonly thought that an incumbent president is at a disadvantage in these debates and on the defensive about well-known blunders and ongoing problems. But the debates between Ford and Carter didn't make much difference to either candidate. Impartial observers gave the first debate on domestic issues to Ford, the second on foreign policy to Carter. And they couldn't agree who won the third. As election day neared, Jimmy's edge in the polls kept slipping. Although people generally considered Jerry Ford to be something of a bumbler who would be forever tied to the wrongdoings of the Nixon administration, the fact was that he was president and people knew him. Jimmy, the outsider, was largely an unknown, and it made many people uncomfortable.

The showdown came on November 2, 1976. As millions of Americans lined up at polling booths to cast their votes for the next president of the United States, Jimmy and his family and friends and aides gathered inside a large suite at Atlanta's Omni Hotel. The atmosphere was chaotic and tense, the vote too close to call. Long after midnight they were all still pacing. Finally, at three o'clock in the morning, the phone rang. It was the governor of Mississippi. The room fell quiet. "We won!" cried Jimmy, the receiver still in his hand. "We won Mississippi! Thank you, Governor. That puts us over the top."

The room went wild. All the tension that had been building over the long months erupted into cheers and tears and bear hugs. True, it had been a narrow electoral college victory. But in the end Jimmy's solid base of support in the South, plus his victories in three big northern states, New York, Pennsylvania, and Ohio, had swung the election. The dream had come true. Jimmy Carter had become the next president of the United States.

Later that night he and Rosalynn left Atlanta and flew home to Plains. The sun was just coming up over the horizon as Jimmy mounted the platform of the old depot to say a few words to his friends who had stayed up to greet him. As he glanced toward the one block of stores and the railroad tracks stretching east toward Americus and west toward the farm where he'd grown up, he had to be aware of the enormous distance he'd gone. It was an emotional moment. The boy from Plains had come home, and there were tears in his eyes.

9

The President from Plains

Despite the bitter cold in Washington on January 20, 1977, thousands of people lined the inaugural parade route, waiting to glimpse Jimmy Carter as the presidential motorcade passed by. The mood in the streets was festive and hopeful. The modest, soft-spoken new president seemed such a positive figure, so different from presidents of the recent past. Being from the Deep South, he seemed to offer a kind of national reconciliation not only between Northerners and Southerners but among Americans everywhere.

Just as the long, black limousine carrying the president started on its way, it stopped. People within its view gasped as they saw Jimmy Carter and his lovely First Lady get out of the car. What was happening? Had the limousine developed motor problems? Smiling and relaxed, the new president took his wife's hand and began walking. Then, as the couple's three sons and their wives and nine-year-old Amy joined them, they began striding briskly from the U.S. Capitol to the White House, a distance of 1.2 miles.

On January 20, 1977, Jimmy Carter is sworn in as the thirty-ninth President of the United States. Rosalynn Carter holds the family Bible for her husband.

The crowds went wild with joy. Never in memory could they recall a time a U.S. president had actually walked during his inaugural parade! Because of security problems in recent years, presidents had always ridden in bulletproof limousines that shielded them from direct contact with the crowds. But Jimmy had wanted to be part of the people. A simple walk, he had felt, would demonstrate his confidence that he was safe among his fellow Americans. More important, it would be a symbol of his determination to reduce the increasing tendency to convey upon a U.S. president and his family a kind of regal status.

After the parade Jimmy and his family were alone briefly. Excitedly they began exploring the White House, their home for the next four years. Although Jack Carter and his family would be moving back to Georgia, everyone else would live here. Jimmy, Rosalynn, and Amy were to occupy the second-floor living quarters; Chip and Jeff and their wives would share the third floor. On the third floor, too, was a nursery for the new baby Chip and Caron were expecting.

In the midst of their tour, the family suddenly realized that Jimmy was missing. Remembering how eager he'd been to visit the Oval Office, they headed toward the West Wing of the White House. There he was, just as they'd suspected, sitting alone behind the president's desk. It was a picture they'd seen thousands of times—the president of the United States behind his desk in the Oval Office framed by the president's flag on one side and the American flag on the other. But this was Jimmy, the man they knew intimately, a man who now would be in charge of the welfare of the nation. They stared at him in silence, momentarily overcome by the soberness of the scene. Jimmy looked up and grinned. But he made no move to get up from his new desk.

It was at this desk that the new president spent most of his time in the coming weeks and months. In the same way that he had always immersed himself in everything he had ever done—the navy, farming, politics—he then threw himself completely into the job of becoming a good president. Probably no president in history, in fact, has ever worked so hard or with such determination to master the maze of complex details that are a part of modern-day government. Rising at five-thirty every morning, he was in the Oval Office by six where he would have his first cup of coffee while reading the morning newspapers as well as the secretary of state's Overnight Report. Regular appointments would begin at eight o'clock and continue throughout the day. Between appointments Jimmy would tackle the mountains of paperwork continually brought to his desk: pages and pages of detailed analysis about

The new President waves to the crowds as he and Amy and Rosalynn walk to the White House during their inaugural parade.

major problems, proposals from cabinet officers that needed his approval, correspondence he had to sign, facts about legislation before Congress, intelligence and defense reports, and on and on. In order to deal with all this more quickly, he arranged to take, along with Rosalynn and several of his key aides, a speed-reading course once a week in the Cabinet Room. It doubled his speed.

For the same reasons that he had decided to walk during his inaugural parade, Jimmy did away with many of the other regal trappings of modern-day presidents. He wanted people to know that he was accessible, one of *them*, just another citizen hired to do the job. To emphasize this, he appeared at his first nationally televised news conference wearing a cardigan sweater and an open-necked shirt rather than a coat and tie. He also banned most of the White House pomp and ceremony. He urged senior government officials to do without limousines and he ordered that the traditional presidential song, "Hail to the Chief," be played only on special occasions rather than every time he appeared in public. Whereas other presidents' children had led sheltered lives in the White House and gone to exclusive private schools, he and Rosalynn sent Amy to a nearby public school where her classmates reflected the economic and racial diversity of people living in the nation's capital.

There were other populist symbols too. Not only did he travel widely in the beginning months of his presidency, but wherever he went, he appeared at local town meetings and stayed overnight in ordinary citizens' houses. To demonstrate that he and his family were not above other families in confronting rising oil costs and in preserving energy, he ordered the White House thermostats to be turned down to sixty-five degrees during the day and to fifty-five at night. Even Rosalynn complained about that, but it did no good. On cold, wintry days she took to wearing long underwear in the White House.

All new presidents can expect to enjoy a "honeymoon" period following their inauguration, a time when every-

The President chats with his and Rosalynn's hosts and their neighbors on an overnight stay in Pittsburgh, PA, in 1979.

one gives them wide support and approval. Jimmy was no exception. The country seemed to love his style and to admire the way he gave himself so completely to the job. Having pledged to restore moral fiber to the government, with more openness and honesty in dealing with the press and the public, he began his presidency by giving two press conferences a month. The press corps was dazzled, amazed that anyone could give such a smooth, candid performance and show such a thorough grasp of even the most complex issues.

Like most presidents, Jimmy was more attracted to foreign policy than to issues facing the nation at home. In broad terms, he had pledged to dedicate himself to the goals of world peace and to nuclear arms control. More specifically, he wanted to complete the signing of the Panama Canal treaties, normalize relations with China, develop closer ties with Latin America, negotiate a SALT II treaty with the Soviet Union, and establish a more creditable U.S. presence in Africa. But the area of the world that concerned him most was the Middle East. The complicated problems and issues there were such a potential threat to peace that he felt that he, himself, must become an expert in Middle Eastern affairs. By the second year of his presidency, he was.

The cornerstone of his foreign policy, however, was his strong, outspoken stand for human rights, something all other recent presidents had ignored. In competing with the Soviet Union, the United States in the past had tended to divide the world into anti-Communists or pro-Communists, friends or enemies. Those countries that espoused an anti-Communist line were automatically friends of the United States and above criticism. Yet frequently some of these friendly nations were run by ruthless dictators who savagely suppressed freedom in their own countries, imprisoning, torturing, and even murdering citizens who disagreed with them. That the United States had blindly tolerated these situations was wrong, Jimmy felt. Why couldn't U.S. foreign policy reflect the morality and idealism of democracy? Why couldn't it uphold the belief that all people are entitled to have their basic human rights respected?

"As president, I hoped and believed that the expansion of human rights might be the norm of the future throughout the world, and I wanted the United States to be on the crest of this movement." Thus, he let it be known that under his administration U.S. dealings with other nations—both friendly and hostile—would be influenced by the way those countries treated their own citizens.

As challenged as Jimmy was by foreign policy, he did not ignore problems at home. Like conservatives, he strongly believed in fiscal responsibility and the elimination of wasteful spending as well as creating a more efficient government bureaucracy. Like liberals, he was genuinely moved by the problems of the poor and the jobless, and he wanted to do more for them. In addition, he wanted welfare

President Jimmy Carter at work in the Oval Office

reform, tax reform, and a less-polluted, more beautiful environment. In fact, he was interested in many things — the plight of the American farmer, the preservation of whales, the nuclear submarine corps, the fate of the American shoe industry, the conservation of water.

Among the problems that Americans faced at home, there was none more serious, Jimmy felt, than the energy crisis. When he took office, U.S. dependency on foreign oil supplies had grown to almost 50 percent of the country's entire consumption. Furthermore, the United States was the only developed nation without an energy policy. The way things were going, it was distinctly possible that supplies of oil and natural gas would not be adequate for U.S. needs in the future.

And so Jimmy spoke to the nation on April 17, 1977:

The energy crisis has not yet overwhelmed us, but it will if we do not act quickly.... Our decision about energy will test the character of the American people and the ability of the president and the Congress to govern this nation. This difficult effort will be the "moral equivalent of war," except that we will be uniting our efforts to build and not to destroy.

Several things needed to be done to confront the crisis. Everyone in the nation had to conserve energy, using less heating oil and driving more energy-efficient cars. The United States needed to begin developing more fuel production at home to free itself from the pressures of potential blackmail from oil-producing nations abroad. Finally, more research into alternative forms of energy, including the sun, needed to begin at once. Jimmy asked for, and got, a new department of energy. To head it, he named James Schlesinger, former CIA chief and secretary of defense.

In launching the ideas and programs of his administration, Jimmy had plenty of help. Like other presidents, he chose those individuals whom he knew best and trusted most for positions on his White House staff. These, of course, were his fellow Georgians. He appointed Hamilton Jordan as chief of staff and Jody Powell as his press secretary. Other Georgians who served in the White House included Frank Moore, his liaison to Congress; Jack Watson, who coordinated his transition to the presidency; and Stuart Eisenstat, who was given responsibility for preparing and monitoring White House legislative proposals for consideration by Congress.

Unlike his White House staff, the nine men and one woman chosen for his cabinet came from all over the United States and were largely people with national reputations as leaders in government, business, law, and education. Jimmy's secretary of state, Cyrus Vance, for instance, was considered an expert in foreign affairs, having formerly served as both secretary of the army and deputy secretary of defense. Harold Brown, whom Jimmy appointed secretary of defense, was a physicist who had been serving as president of the California Institute of Technology.

In addition to his cabinet, cabinet-level positions had to be filled. Jimmy appointed Zbigniew Brzezinski, his former leader on the Trilateral Commission, as national security adviser and chose two longtime friends and supporters from Georgia for other high, cabinet-level jobs. Andrew Young, the black congressman from Atlanta, was named ambassador to the United Nations. Bert Lance, the banker who had served as director of the Georgia Department of Transportation while Jimmy was governor, became the new director of the Office of Management and Budget.

Traditionally U.S. presidents do not have close working relationships with their vice presidents. Despite its prestigious title, the vice presidency is widely considered a rather dull and powerless job, its duties limited to filling in for the president at funerals of leaders from other nations or heading trade councils or special study commissions. But this was not the role that Vice President Mondale played during the Carter administration. From the beginning, Jimmy had wanted his vice president to be truly second-in-command, involved in every aspect of governing. Thus Fritz Mondale attended cabinet meetings, received the same security briefings as did the president, and helped plan strategy for domestic programs, diplomacy, and defense. Not only did Mondale occupy the adjoining office to Carter's in the West Wing, highly unusual in itself, but every Monday the two men had a regularly scheduled lunch together.

Also in contrast to other past presidents, Jimmy relied heavily on his wife's opinions and advice on issues and political strategies. Some first ladies have limited their activities to being wives, mothers, and hostesses. Others, such as Eleanor Roosevelt and Lady Bird Johnson, have used the prestige of the First Family to further worthwhile causes. But having been married thirty-one years, during which time they'd been partners in everything they'd ever done, Jimmy and Rosalynn were an unusually close presidential couple, each involved in whatever concerned the other. Says Jimmy, "We had been ridiculed for allowing our love to be apparent to others. It was not an affectation but was as natural as breathing."

Their sense of partnership went far beyond love and mutual support. Although Rosalynn had her own areas of interest, namely, the problems of the mentally ill, she also sat in on cabinet meetings and regularly received detailed briefings from her husband's domestic and national security staff. Except for a few highly secret and sensitive security matters, Jimmy discussed everything with her. In June 1977 he sent Rosalynn as his envoy to Central America. One of her duties was to urge countries such as Jamaica, Costa Rica, Ecuador, Peru, Brazil, Colombia, and Venezuela to sign the American Convention on Human Rights, a pact guaranteeing human rights in those countries. Her other mission was to urge them to sign a treaty that would prohibit the placement of nuclear weapons in Central and South America. Thus, her visit was not merely a ceremonial, goodwill trip. Unlike other First Ladies, she discussed substantive issues with leaders of these countries and regularly held news conferences.

It is difficult to pinpoint exactly when Jimmy's popularity with the press and the public began to wane. But by midsummer 1977 it was clear that the warmth of the honeymoon had begun to fade. Criticism came first from those who had supported him most. Black leaders started complaining that he had not moved quickly enough to reduce unemployment among young blacks. Charging him with spending too much time on foreign policy, they grumbled that he had been completely insensitive to the needs of the country's minority groups.

Then came a bombshell, one that brought the nation's press into the attack. Bert Lance, Jimmy's close friend from Georgia, began to be suspected of having committed illegal banking practices earlier while president of Georgia's Calhoun National Bank. The furor had started during

The President and his First Lady

Lance's Senate confirmation hearings, normally a routine process for all presidential appointees to determine their eligibility for the job. In assessing his qualifications to head the Office of Management and Budget, the Senate committee had become suspicious that Lance may not have been a model of honesty as a banker.

Throughout that summer and into early fall stories about Bert Lance and his allegedly shady banking practices were featured daily in the nation's news. Some people wanted him fired immediately. But Jimmy wanted to give his old friend a chance to publicly clear his name. By September, although Lance had redeemed himself somewhat at further Senate hearings, it had become clear that the investigation would not cease. In order not to damage the president more than he already had, Bert Lance resigned.

Other presidents have had similar problems when members of their staff or cabinet have been accused of wrongdoing. Following the initial public furor, the matter is usually resolved in time and forgotten. But Jimmy was different from other presidents. Bringing honesty and morality back to government had been a central campaign promise: " . . . a government as good and as honest and as decent" as the American people. And millions of people had believed his words, believed that under his administration the nation would be rid of shabby conduct at high political levels. Now here was one of Jimmy's oldest and best friends from Georgia, resigning under a cloud of suspicion. To many people, the episode seemed a betrayal by the president they wanted to believe in, a sad retreat to politics-as-usual.

"It is impossible to overestimate the damage inflicted on my administration by the charges leveled against Bert Lance," wrote Carter years later.

And he was right.

10

Trials, Troubles, and Treaties

The most important reason for the conflicts between me and Congress was the extremely controversial matters we would have to address....

This day has been a nightmare.... The crucial vote on energy was 207–206.

Diary, October 13, 1978

The issue of water projects was the one that caused the deepest breach between me and the Democratic leadership.

... it now seems that it would have been advisable to have introduced our legislation in much more careful phases—not in such a rush.

The battles with Congress over the Panama Canal treaties and energy had been long, drawn-out, and debilitating...

*...on several issues I failed to gain congressional approval for my proposals. The loss of three in particular—welfare and tax reform and a national health program—were a great disappointment.**

---

*These six quotes are from Jimmy Carter, *Keeping Faith: Memoirs of a President* (New York: Bantam, 1982).

A portrait of President Carter—the burdens of running the government etched on his face.

No matter how brilliant, hardworking, or well-intentioned a president may be, he must have the cooperation of Congress. Otherwise, few of his goals and programs will be realized.

As a presidential candidate, Jimmy had stressed that being an outsider he could bring a fresh approach and new ideas to Washington. Because of the general feeling that politicians in the nation's capital were not to be trusted, this had struck many people as one of the hopeful things about him. As it turned out, however, it was not an advantage. Among Jimmy's own worst memories of being president were his long and tiring battles with Congress. During his four years in office, he failed to forge any strong alliances or friendships on Capitol Hill. As one former Democratic senator said, "There was no one up on the Hill who would go the last mile for him."

Why? There are probably several reasons. Within his own Democratic party were important members of Congress who had fought against him for the party's nomination. Old wounds do not heal easily. And because of Jimmy's conservative position on fiscal matters, some of the more liberal Democrats felt that he didn't reflect their party's ideals, that he was more of a Republican than a Democrat. Beyond that, Jimmy was hard to get to know. Although he could be tireless on the phone with congressional members and brilliant in informal sessions with them, he never made them feel he was entirely comfortable in their midst. It was the same way he had made state legislators in Georgia feel when he was governor. Ever so slightly, he conveyed the impression of moral superiority. It was as if he felt that as president, he, and only he, had a commitment to the welfare of the whole nation, while the others were vulnerable to demands of special interest groups, lobbies, and selfish blocs.

His relations with Congress might have improved, however, had he and his aides understood the way Washington works. The nation's capital is home to thousands of important people, all concerned with the government. Some are influential newspaper publishers and widely read journalists. Others include top foreign diplomats and highly respected elder statesmen who have served past presidents. How do all these people get to know one another?

At parties. The social life in Washington is taken very seriously and is considered almost an extension to running the government. It is at Washington parties that those in power and those out of power as well as those who are the observers of power can meet, get to know one another in a relaxed setting, and exchange ideas. This, in turn, can lead to closer relationships of understanding and support. Yet Jimmy and his fellow Georgians in the White House stood apart from Washington's social life. Even Jimmy admitted later that this aloofness had been a mistake: "We missed an opportunity to become better friends with some good and important people, who never felt that they were wanted or needed in helping to form the policies of our nation."

Perhaps none of this would have mattered if Carter had been the kind of dynamic leader who could have rallied the support of the people against Congress. But that wasn't the case. He was not an eloquent public speaker. Although he could be very impressive when answering questions in televised press conferences, his set speeches seldom succeeded in stirring anyone. Whereas his soft-spoken, gentle manner had charmed people when he was a candidate, that same manner hurt him when he became president because it conveyed a lack of force. And that, in turn, contributed to the growing opinion that he simply was not "presidential."

Other negative factors were the frequent inconsistencies and retreats in his positions. All presidents have some of these, but Jimmy seemed to zigzag in his policies more than most. Early in his presidency, for instance, he had backed a plan to give a tax rebate of fifty dollars to every person in the nation in order to stimulate a stagnant economy. A few months later, he canceled his request, deciding that the rebate would spur inflation. A few months after becoming president, he had banned further development of the B-1 bomber as being unnecessary and too costly. People opposed to massive and unchecked military spending applauded his courage. But later these same people were appalled when he approved plans to develop the neutron bomb, a weapon deadly to all forms of animal life while barely destructive to property. When European leaders resisted the deployment of this bomb in their

Jimmy at the White House signing legislation.

countries, Jimmy quickly backed down, deciding not to go ahead with it after all.

A similar retreat came in 1979 when a Soviet combat brigade was suddenly discovered in Cuba. In his first public statement on the matter, Jimmy spoke forcefully: "We consider the presence of a Soviet combat brigade in Cuba to be a very serious matter and that this status quo is not acceptable." Further investigation, however, revealed that these same Soviet troops had been in Cuba for at least twenty years and were not a threat to the United States. So Jimmy chose to ignore their presence and the matter was dropped. To the public, however, it was another instance of the president shooting from the hip too soon and then backing down.

Yet despite his lack of support from the public or any other sector, Jimmy had an acceptable record for getting his bills through Congress. During his four-year term, according to *Congressional Quarterly* magazine, he won three out of four roll call votes on issues on which he'd taken a strong stand. True, he failed to reform the welfare and tax systems. And he was not able to institute national health insurance or bring down the soaring costs of medical services. Also he was unable to appreciably cut waste in government spending or streamline the federal bureaucracy. But he made big improvements in education, strengthening the control of schools at local levels and tripling the budget for federal student loan programs, enabling more young people to go to college.

Perhaps his greatest achievement among those domestic issues he fought for, was his far-reaching energy program. The struggle for a national energy policy involved an exhausting battle with Congress that consumed his entire term as president. But in the end he prevailed. As a result, the nation was better equipped to deal with periods of energy shortage or oversupply in the future. Most important, Carter can be credited for changing the attitudes of Americans everywhere, making most people realize the absolute necessity of conserving energy.

Foreign policy issues are not so dependent upon the approval of Congress as are domestic issues. Even so, Carter's success in improving U.S. relations with other countries was mixed. On the positive side, he succeeded in normalizing relations with China, a process begun six years earlier by President Nixon and his secretary of state, Henry Kissinger. Under Jimmy's administration, however, agreements for full diplomatic relations were signed. These forwarded trade relations between the two countries and established scientific, technological, and cultural exchanges.

Also on the positive side, Carter successfully engineered the signing of the Panama Canal treaties. Since any treaty

The President presides over an economic meeting at the White House.

between the United States and another country must be ratified by Congress, this involved yet another long and exhausting battle with members of Congress. The background of the proposed Panama Canal treaties involved a very old treaty signed by the two countries in 1903 when the United States had built the Panama Canal. Under its terms, the United States was given not only the right to build, operate, and defend the canal forever, but also complete control of all land surrounding it. With the passage of time, Panamanians had grown increasingly bitter about the U.S. presence in their country. It seemed to them symbolic of U.S. imperialism. In 1964, therefore, President Lyndon Johnson agreed to renegotiate the 1903 treaties, but the negotiations had dragged on because of strong opposition from members of Congress.

"Jimmy Carter is giving away our canal!" became the battle cry of those opposed to the treaties. To them, the issue represented another case of U.S. weakness in the face of unreasonable foreign demands. To Jimmy and other advocates of the treaty, the new agreements were a vital condition for improved relations between the United States and its neighbors in Central and South America. So the struggle went on in Congress for months. For Jimmy the situation was similar to being the central figure in a nonstop juggling act. On one hand, he had to calm the Panamanians continually, keeping them from making unreasonable demands that would offend the U.S. public. On the other, he had to influence U.S. public opinion and constantly persuade members of Congress that the nation's interests would be best served by signing the treaties. In the end he prevailed and the treaties were signed, giving the Panama Canal Zone back to Panama while allowing the United States to continue operating and defending the canal itself until the year 2000.

Unfortunately, the president was not so successful in his dealings with the Soviet Union. When he had come to office, one of his primary goals was to complete an arms control agreement with the USSR limiting the arsenal of nuclear weapons being stockpiled by the two countries. In 1972 an interim agreement, the Strategic Arms Limitation Talks, known as SALT I, had been signed by both nations. Essentially it was an agreement to agree on continuing the arms talks in the immediate future in hope of signing a more permanent pact, one that would be called SALT II.

Under Carter's administration, the talks on SALT II went forward. Secretary of State Cyrus Vance met with

The signing of the Panama Canal Treaty

the Soviets in Geneva in 1978. The following year Carter flew to Vienna, Austria, to meet with Soviet President Leonid Brezhnev. The treaty was signed there, but soon after, while Jimmy and other proponents of SALT II were lobbying throughout the country for the treaty's ratification by the Senate, the Soviet Union invaded Afghanistan. This wiped out any chance of getting the necessary two-thirds vote in the Senate for approval of SALT II. For Jimmy it was a bitter loss. "Our failure to ratify the SALT II Treaty and to secure even more far-reaching agreements on nuclear arms control was the most profound disappointment of my presidency."

From then on, U.S. and Soviet relations deteriorated. The Soviets had already denounced Jimmy's human rights policies, saying it was highly arrogant for the United States to interfere in the Soviet Union's internal policies by criticizing its treatment of its own citizens. In reaction to the Soviet invasion of Afghanistan, Jimmy angrily canceled all further shipments of grain intended for the Soviet Union. As additional punishment he ordered U.S. Olympic athletes to stay away from the 1980 Olympics being held in Moscow the following summer. To many people both inside and out of the United States, this seemed an inappropriate and ultimately harmful measure. The Olympic Games, after all, were a sporting event. Without the intrusion of politics, they had always been an area where nations could compete on a friendly basis.

Although Jimmy's dealings with China, the Soviet Union, and Central and South America consumed his time and energy throughout his presidency, no area of the world commanded so much of his attention as the Middle East. It was there that he received the most fatal blow to his presidency. And it was there, too, that he achieved his most stunning victory.

11

Camp David: "The Jimmy Carter Conference"

One July afternoon in 1978, while Jimmy and Rosalynn were at Camp David, a mountaintop retreat in Maryland used by presidents to escape pressures of the White House, it became clear to Rosalynn that Jimmy had not left all his problems behind. He was worrying about the Middle East. During the first year of his presidency, he had been very hopeful that Egypt's president Anwar Sadat and Israel's prime minister Menachem Begin might put aside their countries' ancient quarrels and begin talks that would lead to a lasting peace in the region. But lately the two leaders had seemed further apart than ever, and peace seemed a distant dream.

"It's so beautiful here," Jimmy mused as he and Rosalynn strolled through the woods. "I don't believe anybody could stay in this place, close to nature, peaceful and isolated from the world, and still carry a grudge. I believe if I could get both Sadat and Begin here together, we could work out some of the problems between them, or at least we could learn to understand each other better and maybe make some progress. Everything's going backward now."

When Jimmy had been elected president, all of his advisers had warned him to stay out of the Middle East situation. The region had too many complex problems, and every conceivable solution had already been tried by past presidents without success. But Jimmy didn't listen. Feeling that the entire Middle East posed a genuine threat to the United States, he was determined to try to find new answers to the problems there.

Following World War II, which had brought such devastation to the Jews, many nations had wanted to provide the Jewish people with a homeland, a place they could call their own. In 1947 the UN General Assembly had voted to partition the British section of Palestine into a Jewish and an Arab state. The Jewish state was called Israel. The only problem was that most Arabs in the region refused to acknowledge Israel's right to exist. Despite four wars with their neighbors, however, the Israelis survived. And throughout all those years the United States had always been their best friend.

Israel's existence, however, had made refugees of hundreds of thousands of Arabs from Palestine. Some had left when Israel became a nation; others had moved following Israel's defeat of Egypt in the Six Day War of 1967. For almost ten years, this latter group of refugees, as well as the Palestinian Arabs who had remained in their homes on the West Bank, had been living under Israeli military rule without any rights of their own.

Clearly the issue of Palestinian rights was an important one. Equally important was Israel's right to exist as a nation. But since the Arabs didn't recognize Israel as a nation, and the Israelis didn't recognize the Palestinian Liberation Organization (PLO) as the leading representative of the Palestinian Arabs, there had never been any direct communication between the two. And so, the potentially explosive questions remained unanswered: Who owned the land, Jews or Arabs? What were the rights of the Palestinian Arabs? And how could Israel's security be guaranteed when it was totally surrounded by hostile neighbors?

In the beginning months of his presidency, Jimmy had seen a glimmer of hope in the situation. Egypt, Israel's strongest and most formidable foe, had broken its close ties with the Soviet Union. At this time Egypt was considered neutral, even rather friendly toward the United States. Moreover Egypt had begun to hint at a more moderate attitude toward Israel.

Three months after Carter's inauguration, Egypt's president Anwar Sadat had paid a courtesy call on the new American president in Washington. The two leaders instantly liked and trusted each other. In their lengthy talks about problems in the Middle East, it was clear to Carter that Sadat genuinely wanted to end the stalemate in that region. And with his wisdom and boldness, he seemed just the man to do it. When the two men parted, Sadat promised Carter that, at a crucial moment, he would support him in their common quest for peace in the Middle East.

One by one other Arab leaders came to Washington—first, King Hussein of Jordan, then President Hafez Assad of Syria, next Crown Prince Fahd of Saudi Arabia. Although their sympathies were for their fellow Arabs, the Palestinians, each of them pledged support for Carter's peace effort. Jimmy knew, however, that unlike Sadat, none of them would be willing to take the initiative in any peace efforts.

Israel's newly elected prime minister, Menachem Begin, arrived in Washington in the summer of 1977. A complicated, brilliant man, he had suffered a great deal in his own life because of the persecution of the Jews. As a former right-wing, radical leader in Israel, he was considered to have rigid, nonconciliatory views toward the Arabs and a determination to keep Israel the strongest nation in the Middle East. Although he longed for peace, his distrust of Israel's neighbor nations was so deeply ingrained that it made prospects for successful peace talks extremely dim.

Still Carter went forward, trying to get the Arab countries and Israel to come to a multinational United Nations peace conference in Geneva, Switzerland. But Israel and the other Middle Eastern nations couldn't even agree on the guidelines for a Geneva conference or on such details as who should or should not attend. Feeling utterly discouraged, Jimmy wrote a personal letter to Anwar Sadat, reminding him of his promise of support at a crucial moment in their common search for peace. In response Sadat announced to the Egyptian parliament that he would be willing to go to Jerusalem in Israel.

In November 1977 at the invitation of Begin, Sadat made good on his word. Not only did he visit Jerusalem, but he made a dramatic speech to the Knesset, Israel's parliament, outlining Arab requirements for any peace settlement. It was an emotional moment for Israel. As Sadat stood alone, holding out an olive branch of peace to a people who had been Egypt's enemy for centuries, they welcomed him with tears and cheers. Sadat's courage at last seemed to have broken the solid Arab shell that had isolated Israel for so long.

The other Arab nations, however, were furious about Sadat's visit. Syria immediately broke diplomatic relations with Egypt. High officials in the Syrian, Libyan, and Iraqi governments called for Sadat's assassination, and prospects for peace again looked remote. But Jimmy continued working toward that goal. Yet, despite his separate meetings with Sadat and Begin, despite his and other U.S. officials' visits to the Middle East, the peace effort began losing ground. What's more, even Anwar Sadat, who had become increasingly isolated from his former Arab allies, had begun to give up. He felt that Prime Minister Begin was so determined to build up Israel's strength and power in the Middle East that he couldn't possibly want peace.

It was in this climate of hostility that Jimmy made up his mind to make one last effort. He invited Anwar Sadat and Menachem Begin to meet with him at Camp David. Both leaders immediately and eagerly accepted the invitation.

Most of Jimmy's closest friends and advisers had been strongly opposed to such a meeting, for it was an astounding idea, one that ignored the most basic rules of diplomacy. Usually when countries begin negotiations, the long, tedious preliminaries are carried on by lower-level officials. If agreements cannot be reached, as is often the case, the leaders themselves emerge unscarred and better able to initiate further negotiations in the future.

Jimmy knew he was taking an enormous political risk. If the Camp David talks failed, he would be the one blamed. Yet as he listened to his advisers warn him against such a meeting, he became more determined to go ahead. "No one, including me, could think of a specific route to success, but everyone could describe a dozen logical scenarios for failure—and all were eager to do so. I slowly became hardened against them, and as stubborn as at any other time I can remember."

And so, on September 5, 1978, President Sadat of Egypt and Prime Minister Begin of Israel arrived separately at Camp David where they were greeted by President Carter of the United States. A Jew, an Arab, and a Christian—the leaders of three nations—had come to isolate themselves from the outside world in the hope of bringing harmony to the Middle East. Before their arrival, they had agreed to talk for at least three days, and no longer than a week. Little did any of them suspect that they would remain at Camp David for thirteen exhausting and discouraging days. But problems between Egypt and Israel defied easy solutions. As Begin reminded Carter when he arrived, there had not been an agreement between a Jewish nation and Egypt for more than two thousand years.

Sadat, Begin, and Carter occupied the three main lodges at Camp David, located less than a hundred yards from one another. Each leader had his own doctor, his own secretarial staff, and his own communication facilities for conducting the long-distance affairs of his government. In addition, there were cooks at the camp who specialized in preparing Egyptian, American, and kosher foods. Finally, because of limited space, each leader held to a specified number of expert advisers and aides to help with the negotiating.

The talks began on a bad note. President Sadat, the leader whom Jimmy had counted on to be the more flexible of the two, presented a plan for peace that was rigid and uncompromising. Begin was furious. "This smacks of a victorious state dictating peace to the defeated! ... This document is not a proper basis for negotiations." On the third day, at two separate meetings of the three leaders, Begin and Sadat were brutal toward each other, exchanging harsh words. On the morning of the fourth day, Jimmy received word that Sadat had given up, that he was packing to leave Camp David. Begin, meanwhile, was just as disgusted. It was rumored that he had begun preparing a public statement giving his reasons why the talks had failed.

Quickly and desperately, Carter swung into action. First he requested a meeting with Begin; then he scheduled a meeting with Sadat. He suggested to both men that rather than Egypt or Israel presenting its own plans for peace, the United States would draft a proposal that would take into consideration the interests of both countries. Although Begin was unhappy about the idea, he agreed reluctantly. So did Sadat, who trusted Jimmy. "You write it," he told the American president. "You know the issues that are important to me. I will support any reasonable document you put forth."

The American Team, headed by President Carter, works late into the night at Camp David on peace proposals.

During the weekend of September 9 and 10, all efforts went into drafting the American plan, called a Framework for Peace. The plan was then presented separately to both countries. By that time Sadat and Begin were neither seeing nor talking to each other. But they were both seeing Jimmy Carter, communicating through him with each other. Often Carter's sessions with the two leaders and their advisers would last well into the night. The American document would be scrutinized by the Israelis, who would make their changes, then it would go to the Egyptians, who would add or delete things. Back and forth the document went with additions, changes, deletions, drafts, and redrafts. Sometimes tempers would flare and the talks would threaten to end. But largely through Jimmy's efforts, the air would clear and the slow, painful progress toward peace would begin again.

Both Sadat and Begin worked until they were exhausted. But Carter worked twice as hard as the go-between, the one who had to attend meetings of both countries. Indeed, the Camp David talks were pretty much his show. Here, his determination, his capacity for hard work, his fine intelligence, his sense of morality, and his vast appetite

Although exhausted, President Carter beams as Israeli Prime Minister Begin (right) and Egyptian President Sadat (left) successfully conclude their peace talks.

for detail paid off. He knew thoroughly the problems of the Middle East. He had a shrewd sense of what was not negotiable, and he had the vision to fit into a larger plan what was immediately attainable. Not only was he tough when he needed to be, but he demonstrated the patience and stamina to outlast both Begin and Sadat.

There were times, though, when even he was ready to give up. One such moment came on the eleventh day. By then major concessions had been made by both countries and the remaining differences didn't seem too severe. Yet suddenly the final negotiations came to an impasse. Heartbroken, Carter called together the American team to discuss the best ways that the three nations could announce their failure to the world.

Suddenly Secretary of State Vance appeared, his face ashen. "Sadat is leaving," he said. "He and his aides are already packed. He asked me to order him a helicopter."

Carter went directly to Sadat. He pleaded with him to stay, to try again for an agreement with Begin. If no agreement was possible, he argued, then at least all three leaders should leave Camp David together in some semblance of harmony. Because of his friendship and respect for the American president, finally Sadat wearily agreed to remain a little longer.

And so the negotiations continued. Time and again in those final days and hours victory would appear near and then abruptly fade. Either the Egyptians or the Israelis would back off, objecting to some fine point in the language used in the document or to some other little thing. The wrangling continued into the thirteenth day. Then suddenly Begin broke the stalemate, agreeing to the final point under dispute. That did it! At last they had a document acceptable to both nations. The impossible had come true.

That evening Carter, Begin, and Sadat flew to Washington in one helicopter. When they stepped out onto the South Lawn of the White House, they were beaming. Inside the White House, they signed the document and held a press conference. "Dear friend," said Sadat to Carter as the TV cameras rolled, " ...you have been most courageous when you took the gigantic step of convening this meeting. The challenge was great, and the risks were high, but so was your determination." Prime Minister Begin was equally lavish in his praise: "The Camp David conference should be renamed. It was the Jimmy Carter conference."

Indeed it was. By almost everyone's standards, the agreement reached there was a major piece of statecraft and a remarkable accomplishment. Although it would take many more months before the final peace treaty between Egypt and Israel was signed, it never would have happened without Carter's efforts. In short, Camp David was the finest hour of Jimmy Carter's presidency.

12

The Final Year

The warm outpouring of public approval for Jimmy's accomplishment at Camp David did not last. By the summer of 1979, grumbling could be heard across the nation. Prices were rising and, in the South, farmers were facing a severe drought. Because of the energy shortage, people everywhere were having to endure long lines at gas stations to get fuel for their cars.

To try again to get Congress to pass the necessary energy legislation, Carter called together a group of distinguished citizens for advice. One of the suggestions that came from that meeting was that of making a few changes in the cabinet. It would signal to the public a fresh start—a good way to turn around the national mood of pessimism.

All presidents must make changes in their staff and their cabinet from time to time. Usually the reshuffling is done quietly and announced later as an accomplished fact. But Jimmy proposed to his cabinet that everyone should resign and that he would accept resignations only of a few. When this news was leaked to the press, the proposed cabinet changes caused a furor. In the end, five cabinet members were replaced. But instead of restoring the public's confidence in Carter's leadership, the

One bright spot in 1980: The Winter Olympics victory of the amazing U.S. hockey team. President Carter welcomes them to the White House.

widely publicized changes had the opposite effect, making Jimmy look impetuous, as if he were blaming his problems on his cabinet and no longer had a firm hand on the government.

Nor did the situation improve. During the next twelve months one crisis followed another. It was in November 1979 that the Americans were taken hostage in Iran, and in December that the Soviet Union had invaded Afghanistan, sabotaging hopes for the SALT II disarmament agreement. The embargo on grain sales to the USSR had followed, making farmers in the Midwest very unhappy. Withdrawal from the 1980 summer Olympics in Moscow had led to further criticism of the president and then in April 1980 the disastrous hostage rescue attempt had failed, leading to the immediate resignation of Secretary of State Vance, who had opposed the mission. This was followed in May 1980 by the arrival of boatloads of Cubans, many of whom were hardened criminals let out of prisons by Fidel Castro and dumped on American shores. As if this wasn't enough, in July 1980 the president's brother, Billy, was put under investigation for allegedly representing Libyan interests in the United States without registering as a foreign agent.

Politically these crises could not have come at a worse time, for 1980 was an election year. Millions of Americans had begun to think about the man they would vote for in the upcoming presidential election.

Carter's two main competitors for the 1980 Democratic party nomination were Senator Edward Kennedy of Massachusetts and Governor Jerry Brown of California. Both had announced their candidacy in November 1979, the same week that the hostages had been taken captive in Iran. All national crises tend at first to bring out enormous public support and approval for an incumbent president, and the tense situation in Iran was no exception. It left both Brown and Kennedy in a predicament. How could they attack Carter in the midst of a national emergency when the entire country was rallying behind the president?

In December, Carter announced his candidacy for a second term. Because of the hostage situation, however, he let it be known that he would not barnstorm the country in search of votes. Instead he planned to remain near the Situation Room in the White House, ready to respond to any message from Iran about the release of the hostages. At the annual White House tree-lighting ceremony that Christmas, the crowds gasped when Amy pulled the switch and the tree remained dark except for the large star on top. Jimmy explained: "On top of the great Christmas tree is a star of hope. We will turn on the lights when our hostages come home, safe and free."

Although Carter remained in Washington during the early months of the campaign, other members of the family did not. Even before 1979 had ended, Rosalynn and Lillian and the Carter sons and their wives had begun campaigning. In an early straw vote in Florida, Jimmy had beaten Kennedy. But Ted Kennedy had discounted that victory, saying he hadn't spent enough time in Florida. According to Kennedy, the Iowa primary would be the first real test between himself and Carter. Opponents began questioning the president's absence from the campaign, inferring that he was a coward "hiding in the Rose Garden."

The attack backfired. Carter won the Iowa primary overwhelmingly, beating his opponents in ninety-nine out of a hundred counties. But Kennedy, though discouraged, stayed in the race. Following the failed rescue mission in Iran in April, Carter's public approval ratings surged. People felt that at least he had tried, at least he had done something, and they rallied behind him. In midspring Jimmy entered the campaign. With sanctions imposed against the Soviets, the Iranian negotiations at a stalemate, and the rescue mission over, there seemed no reason for him to stay strictly at home. By early June he had won enough delegates in the primaries to assure him his party's nomination.

The long primary battles with Kennedy had hurt though. In an effort to patch up their differences and to unify their party, Carter invited Kennedy to meet with him at the White House. Kennedy, however, was not about to drop out of the race and support Carter. Citing "unresolved differences" between the president and himself, he said that he planned to continue fighting all the way onto the convention floor.

The Democratic convention opened in New York on August 11. By then the Republicans had chosen their standard-bearer — the former Hollywood film star and ex-governor of California, Ronald Reagan. And a surprisingly popular choice he was too. As Carter went into the Democratic convention, he trailed Reagan in the polls by a whopping 25 percent. Furthermore, Kennedy was still at his heels, calling for Carter's pledged delegates to abandon the president so that the party could have an "open convention." But this never happened. Carter's delegates stuck with him, thereby assuring him the nomination. What's more, despite the feuding between the Kennedy forces and those who backed Carter, Jimmy's popularity rose among voters in general. By the end of the convention, he was trailing Reagan by only 7 percent.

Carter had been delighted when Ronald Reagan was chosen as his opponent. Of all the Republican candidates, he had thought Reagan would be the easiest to beat. As he later said, " ... it seemed inconceivable that he would be acceptable as president when his positions were exposed clearly to the public." Indeed the two men could not have been more different in their political views.

Reagan was against SALT II and, for that matter, against any nuclear arms agreement with the Soviets. He was also against Carter's human rights policy, against the Panama Canal treaties, and against normalization of relations with China. In addition, he was against environmental protection laws and against the proposed Equal Rights Amendment (ERA) for women. In short, Reagan represented the views of the extreme conservatives in his party, another reason for thinking that he didn't have a chance at being elected president. History had shown that the public votes for presidents whose views are moderate, rejecting candidates who espouse views either too far to the Left or to the Right.

But neither history nor Carter had counted on the sheer force of Reagan's personality and style. He was the perfect candidate for the "television age"—handsome, manly and sure of himself. As a former movie star, he was at ease in front of crowds of thousands or before the bright lights of a television studio. In public appearances he projected an aura of calm and steadiness, warmth and good humor, strength and optimism. The public even forgave his frequent flubs because he was so likable, so reassuring. Whereas Carter talked about restraints, making do with less energy, cutting down on consumer spending, using patience in dealing with the hostage situation, Reagan spoke of an expanding America with more spending money, more jobs, more individual freedom, more forcefulness abroad. People liked what he said. It reminded them of the

President Carter with his family, his aides, and members of his cabinet after being declared his party's nominee for a second term as President in August, 1980.

way America used to be when its problems were less complex and its horizons limitless.

Meanwhile the Democratic party was fractured. Carter had been badly hurt by his long battle with Kennedy. Into the breech stepped Representative John Anderson. In the spring Anderson had launched his "National Unity Campaign," hoping to attract both dissatisfied Democrats and Republicans to his third-party presidential candidacy. In the fall campaign, however, it was not Republicans who abandoned Reagan for Anderson. It was former Kennedy supporters and liberal Democrats, those who otherwise would have supported the president.

Going into the last week of the campaign, Carter was still trailing Reagan, but his polls showed the weekend before the election that he'd nearly caught up. Jimmy was hopeful; Rosalynn firmly believed he would win. On Sunday, two days before the election, Warren Christopher of the State Department had encouraging news on another front: The Iranian parliament had agreed to four crucial points that the United States had insisted upon in negotiations for the release of the hostages. Could it be that this was the breakthrough everyone had been waiting for, and that then the Americans would be sent home? The answer was no, not quite yet. There was still negotiating to do.

As luck would have it, election day happened to coincide with the first anniversary of the capture of the hostages. All over the country on that Monday and Tuesday before and during the election, the press enumerated the sad events of the hostages' fifty-two-week captivity. Suddenly Patrick Caddell, Jimmy's polster, began to get disturbing results from his public opinion polls. Carter was slipping badly. Apparently undecided voters were moving toward Reagan.

The election took place on Tuesday, November 4. Rosalynn arrived home in Plains at two in the morning that day, after a final campaign swing through Wisconsin, Illinois, Missouri, and Alabama. Jack was there to greet her. In the

The Carter family in 1980. Standing left to right: Annette, Jeff, Chip, Allie M. Smith (Rosalynn's mother), the President, Amy holding Jason's hand, Rosalynn, Jack and Judy, holding Sarah. Seated left to right: grandson James and Jimmy's mother, Lillian.

stillness of the darkened house, the truth finally hit her. "We're going to lose," she said numbly to her son.

"I know, Mom. I came back tonight so you wouldn't be all by yourself."

Jimmy did not reach Plains from the West Coast until seven-thirty that morning. Exhausted, he looked at his wife and smiled, realizing that she'd finally faced the probability of defeat. Composing themselves for the television cameras, they got into the car to go vote.

"How bad is it?" Rosalynn asked.

Jimmy made a downward thrust with his thumbs. "It's gone," he said quietly. "It's all over."

Early that evening in Washington, they learned how bad it really was. Ronald Reagan was winning everywhere. Ultimately Jimmy lost all but five states. Except for Georgia, even the South lined up solidly behind Reagan. The voters had spoken loud and clear. They did not want Jimmy Carter to be their president for a second term.

Losing a presidential election is one thing. Clearly it is painful. But probably nothing in politics is as devastating and humiliating as the voters' rejection of a president after a single term. As hurt as Jimmy was, however, he did his best not to show it. He knew he couldn't allow himself to wallow in self-pity. Reagan's inauguration would not take place for another two and a half months. Meanwhile he was still president.

Indeed in the coming weeks, Carter accomplished a great deal. Concerned about making the transition from his administration to Reagan's as smooth as possible, he invited the president-elect to the White House to discuss sensitive national issues. He oversaw the preparation of a national budget for the following year. And he had the satisfaction of seeing Congress pass the remaining points of his energy program. Finally he succeeded in getting Congress to pass two important environmental protection laws—one that dealt with cleaning up toxic wastes and one that permanently protected a hundred and fifty million acres of wilderness land in Alaska.

On January 14, 1981, Jimmy delivered his farewell address to the nation. He spoke of three issues that he felt would be America's primary concerns in the future: the threat of nuclear destruction, the need to preserve the earth's fragile natural resources, and the importance of America's role in upholding basic human rights of people everywhere. He also spoke about a subject that had plagued his presidency for more than a year, one that had become almost an obsession to him:

> I will continue as I have the last fourteen months to work and to pray for the lives of the American hostages held in Iran. I cannot predict yet what will happen, but I hope you will join me in my constant prayer for their freedom.

The President and his advisors monitoring the tense, final negotiations for the release of the American hostages in Iran. January, 1981

During the first two weeks of January, the messages from Iran had suddenly become increasingly positive. Would an agreement finally be reached so that the hostages could come home? By Sunday, January 18, the news was even better. Algerian planes were standing by, ready to fly into Iran to pick up the hostages. Jimmy believed that the long ordeal with Iran had been the undoing of his presidency. More than anything, he wanted the hostages freed while he was still president. In fact, in the two remaining days before the inauguration, he fervently hoped that there would be enough time for him to fly to Wiesbaden, Germany, to greet them.

Carter did not go to bed at all during the last forty-eight hours he was president. He stayed in the Oval Office, monitoring the maze of final negotiating details with the Iranians. At 2:00 A.M. on Monday the news came: Iran had signed the agreements. Everyone in the Oval Office broke into cheers. It was done! Now it was only a matter of waiting for the Algerian planes to take off from the airport in Tehran with the hostages aboard. Jimmy instructed his valet to pack a bag for him to take to Wiesbaden.

The hours ticked on. Still the hostages remained in Iran. Why the delay? Jimmy and his aides kept waiting. Finally it was inauguration day — too late for him to go to Germany. At 8:00 A.M. that morning, word came through: the Algerian plane was ready to take off with all the hostages on board. But in a final act of meanness, the Iranians kept the plane waiting on the ground. Clearly they wanted to make sure that the hostages would not be freed while Jimmy Carter was still president.

And so, moments after Ronald Reagan became president, Jimmy Carter finally heard what he'd been waiting for. Secret Service radios notified him that the first Algerian plane had taken off from Iran at 12:33 P.M., with the second plane following after nine minutes. "I was over-whelmed with happiness, but because of the hostages' freedom, not mine," Jimmy said later.

Jimmy and Rosalynn with Press Secretary Jody Powell (rear center)

That afternoon Air Force One took off from Washington with Jimmy and his family and his closest aides aboard. When he'd lost the election, there had been no hesitancy about where he and Rosalynn would go next. They would go back to the place where he'd once dreamed all those impossible dreams that had led him to becoming president of the United States. They would go home, naturally, to Plains.

Afterword

In the years since President Carter had resumed life as a private citizen, the world has seen and heard little of him. Unlike other ex-presidents, he doesn't play in celebrity golf tournaments and he seldom appears at glittery ceremonial dinners. At the 1984 Democratic convention, where his vice president, Walter Mondale, was nominated for president, the delegates listened politely to his speech. But they did not greet their former president with the rip-roaring enthusiasm usually accorded to beloved party figures. Even Mondale seemed uneasy about his close association with his former boss. It was as if he hoped the public would forget about his role in the Carter administration.

How will history judge Jimmy Carter? Less than a decade after his presidency, it is too early to tell. Jimmy's own favorite president was Harry Truman, whom he described as "decent and honest, somewhat old-fashioned in his attitudes, bound close to his hometown roots, courageous in facing serious challenges, and willing to be unpopular if he believed his actions were best for the country." Although Truman was not overwhelmingly popular as president or in the years immediately thereafter, people increasingly began realizing, as time passed, how often his controversial decisions had been right. Three decades after his unpopular presidency had ended, he was being

Former President Carter working to help make an abandoned building liveable in New York City.

referred to as one of the truly great leaders of this century. It seems likely that the same thing could happen to ex-President Carter.

Since Carter's return to Plains, he has lived a quiet, modest, and rather contemplative life. At first he and Rosalynn were faced with some debts their business had incurred while he was president. Since then, they have sold Carter's Warehouse. During his first year as a private citizen, Carter worked day and night to complete his memoirs. The book, now published, is an open, honest, even self-critical evaluation of the successes and failures of his presidency. He has also been busy raising money and planning his own presidential library in Atlanta. Here scholars will have use of more than twenty-five million documents, letters, memos, and files from his administration. In addition, he has helped launch the Carter Center of Emory University where he and other leaders can meet to continue tackling problems that face the world.

The same genuine goodness and compassion for others that characterized him as president are evident in his life now. Among the causes he has become involved in is a little-known organization called Habitat for Living. Located in nearby Americus, Georgia, Habitat is a nonprofit Christian community that helps people all over the world to become homeowners who otherwise could not afford to own a house. This is accomplished in many cases by Habitat's buying dilapidated buildings cheaply and fixing them up with the help of the prospective owner. Two summers in a row, Jimmy and Rosalynn have traveled to New York City with members of this group. There New Yorkers have been treated to the unusual sight of their former president and his wife laboring as carpenters in one of the city's formerly abandoned buildings.

In his spare time Jimmy indulges his passions for fly-fishing and woodworking. Along with another couple who are close friends, he and Rosalynn have built a log cabin in the north Georgia mountains for which Jimmy designed and built most of the furniture. Sadly, Jimmy's mother, "Miss Lillian," and his sister Ruth, have both died since he left Washington. But the rest of the family thrives. Amy has grown into a bright and independent young lady. And Jimmy and Rosalynn have become grandparents several times over.

For all the compensations of private life, however, it is clear that Jimmy misses being president. "Even when I

The former President with two of his grandchildren.

had my most disappointing days...I don't remember a single morning when I didn't look forward to getting to the Oval Office," he has said. "I enjoyed the challenge of it—analyzing complicated issues, trying to put a plan into effect...overcoming a difficulty...." Even more than his enjoyment of the job, however, he would have liked a second term so that more of his goals might have been realized.

Meanwhile there are accomplishments that he can look back on with satisfaction. In foreign affairs, the Camp David agreement continues to offer hope that the problems of the Middle East are not insolvable. In domestic affairs, his energy program has had far-reaching effects on the way millions of Americans now view the nation's fragile energy resources. Again in foreign affairs, his strong stand for human rights, though controversial, still represents to millions of people the world over the best in the American people.

Jimmy's final visitor in the Oval Office was Max Cleland, a Vietnam veteran and triple amputee. He presented the outgoing president with a plaque which had been inscribed with a quote from Thomas Jefferson: "I have the consolation to reflect that during my administration not a drop of the blood of a single citizen was shed by the sword of war."

And perhaps that was the greatest accomplishment of the president from Plains. He managed to keep the peace during difficult times.

INDEX

Habitat for Living, 120
Honolulu, Hawaii, 33
Humphrey, Hubert, 72
Hurst, Joe, 48, 49
Hussein, King of Jordan, 99
Iowa caucuses, 67, 68
Iranian crisis, 1–11, 107, 108,
    112, 116; rescue effort, 6–11,
    109
Jackson, Henry, 67, 70
Jefferson, Thomas, 122
Jerusalem, Israel, 100
Johnson, Lady Bird, 83
Johnson, Lyndon, 50, 94
Jordan, Hamilton, 9, 62, 67, 82
Kennedy, Edward, 61, 108–110
Kennedy, John F., 72
Khomeini, Ayatollah, 3, 5
Kirbo, Charles, 48, 52, 61
Lance, Bert, 61, 83; suspected
    banking practices of, 84, 86
Maddox, Lester, 52, 53, 56
"Marching Through Georgia," 25
McGovern, George, 61, 62, 63
Mondale, Walter (Fritz), 9, 70,
    83, 118
Moore, Frank, 61, 82
Moscow, U.S.S.R., 96, 107
Muskie, Edmund, 61
National Press Club, 64
National Unity Campaign. See
    John Anderson
New London, Conn., 32, 34, 36
New Orleans, La., 42–43
New York, N.Y., 70, 109, 120
New York Times, 58
Niebuhr, Reinhold, 69
1980 Olympics, withdrawal
    from, 96, 107
Nixon, Richard M., 63, 66, 72,
    92
Norfolk, Va., 29, 30, 31
Pace, Stephen, 20, 23
Palestinian Liberation Army
    (PLO), 98
Panama Canal treaties, 87,
    92–94, 110
Peanut Brigade, 68
Peres, Shimon, 1
Plains, Ga., 11, 14, 16, 20, 24,
    26, 27–28, 31, 32, 37, 38,

39–40, 43, 53, 56, 72, 73,
    113, 119, 122
Powell, Jody, 9, 61–62, 82
Quitman Co., Ga., 48
Ratliff, Eloise, 22, 23, 61
Reagan, Ronald, 109, 110,
    113–14, 116
Republican Party, 50, 51
Rickover, Hyman G., 34–37
Rockefeller, David, 62
Sadat, Anwar, 97, 99, 100–105.
    See also Jimmy Carter, Camp
    David peace talks and
Sanders, Carl, 55
Savannah, Ga., 16
Schenectady, N.Y., 36
Schlesinger, James, 82
Six Day War, 98
Soviet Union, 94–96; invasion
    of Afghanistan by, 96, 107
Strategic Arms Limitation Talks,
    94–96, 107, 110
Strauss, Robert, 63
Tehran, Iran, 1, 6, 8, 116
Time, 58
Tolstoy, Leo, 20
Trilateral Commission, 62, 83
Truman, Harry, 118
United Nations, 5, 83
United States Congress, 43, 52,
    53, 63, 78, 88, 89, 94, 114
United States Naval Academy,
    18, 20, 23, 25, 26, 29, 30, 31
United States Navy, 16, 29, 30,
    34
United States Senate, 96
USS K-1, 34
USS New York, 25, 26
USS Pomfret, 32–33, 34
Vance, Cyrus, 9, 82, 105, 107
Vaught, James, 7, 9–10
Vienna, Austria, 96
Waldheim, Kurt, 5
Washington, D.C., 10, 33, 34,
    35, 58, 63, 64, 65, 72, 88, 99,
    105, 117, 120
Watergate break-in, 66
Wiesbaden, Germany, 116
World War I, 14, 20
World War II, 23, 30, 98
Young, Andrew, 63